Platform Wars 2020!

Do You Know What *Your* Party Is Up To?

Larry Judson Butler

Diablosabe Publishing

Livingston, TX

Copyright © 2020

'When people show you who they are,
believe them the first time.

- Maya Angelou

LIES

Table of Contents

Preface

This is not a completely objective and unbiased examination of party platforms. Instead, I offer you an admittedly subjective viewpoint for your consideration. You wouldn't want me to keep my biases a secret, so here's a short list.

First, I believe that a party's platform *actually means something.* It's worth reading and understanding. Our founding fathers created a framework consisting of three branches of government, and carefully defined how each one should work. But they failed to protect these institutions from a shadowy, over-arching system of control we know today as the two-party system. Political parties are just private clubs, they each represent very different constituencies - and they literally control who runs the government and what they do with their power. So pay attention to party platforms, because they actually tell us what they're going to do to our country.

I also believe that political parties are much more easily corrupted - *and corrected* - than the institutions of the federal government. If we're going to change the country - *or keep it from changing* - we've got to use the power of our party to do it. Without the power of a political party, no public policy proposal would see the light of day. Sure, both parties are big and cumbersome - but not nearly as big and cumbersome as the government institutions they control.

I'm pissed at both parties. I believe that the Republican Party - *the GOP* - has been systematically eaten alive by corporate capitalism and its army of lobbyists. And while its interests are *decidedly not* the interests of real people, corporate capital has cultivated a garden of single-issue voters whose support is ensured by conferring a modicum of power upon the religious right, gun enthusiasts, white nationalists, conspiracy theorists, and xenophobes.

Yeah, I'm pissed at *both parties.* I believe that the Democratic Party talks a good game but has failed to deliver on its promises to be the party of regular, real people. They flirt with the very corporate capitalists that fund the GOP, just for the privilege of using their money in a doomed effort to increase the power of the Party. They recognize that big money created and continues to promote the agenda of the GOP, but they seem entirely ignorant of the fact that the very same money is used to *undermine* the Democratic Party's agenda. All the money has to do is just get itself inside the Party. And it does.

But as biased as I am, you'll find a disciplined approach to evaluating the party platforms. Where policy planks are discussed, they are quoted verbatim. And while the comparison and contrast is necessarily my own, you'll have the opportunity to draw your own interpretation using the original text. But make no mistake - *I'm promoting my own views.*

So if you expected to see dispassionate objectivity here, return the book now and get your money back. But if you can handle opinions that may challenge your own, read on. And leave your responses, arguments, and comments here...

https://larryjudsonbutler.com/

I welcome your responses. After all, I'm still learning; come learn with me.

Introduction

Four years ago, I published *Platform Wars!* in an effort to share my own discoveries as I compared and contrasted the Republican and Democratic platforms. In keeping with long-standing practice, both parties had published detailed platforms. Throughout the primaries and into the general election season, some candidates and their campaigns pursued personal attacks against their opponents to the political death. In a turbulent political environment roiled by racism, xenophobia, nationalism, and personal rancor, platforms seemed to reflect a measure of the stabilizing influence of veteran party operatives.

The validity of a party's platform is tested when the party wins big. Control of both houses of Congress and the White House provides an opportunity to implement policy initiatives - an opportunity limited only by the largesse of big donors and the winds of public opinion. The sincerity of a party's values and beliefs is proven or disproven for all to see. In 2016 the GOP won big. As we review their platform we'll examine the degree to which it was implemented in legislation, administration, and public policy.

The Republican Party did not publish a platform in 2020. This omission stands out in stunning contrast to the pattern established by both parties and maintained throughout their histories. *No major American political party had failed to publish its platform in the last 180 years.* [1]

We'll examine some of the reasons for this failure, and some of its implications for public policy. We'll take the GOP at its word - that their 2016 Platform will be carried forward unchanged - even in a world utterly transformed by the monumental events of the last four years. But while glaring anachronisms will unavoidably taint the comparisons and contrasts we draw between the platforms and between the parties, these anachronisms may themselves help explain the Party's decision to recycle their old platform.

You may notice some minor inconsistencies between the quotations contained in this book and the text of the final platform of the Democratic Party. The draft platform of July 27, 2020 was the primary resource used for this book, and although it was checked for consistency with the final document, minor differences might exist.

[1] https://www.presidency.ucsb.edu/documents/presidential-documents-archive-guidebook/national-political-party-platforms

Understanding Platforms

What Are Platforms?

Political parties function largely within a four-year cycle culminating in the presidential election. Every cycle brings a detailed manifesto of the party's values and beliefs together with statements of proposed policies. These statements are known as planks. This written manifesto serves to guide candidates and provide continuity for the party.

Political parties are like people. They're a little mixed up, and they're not always what they appear to be. They have inner conflicts, ideals, and goals. They're influenced by things going on around them, and they have a powerful instinct for survival. They can sometimes get sick, just like you and me, and even have been known to die.

A party's platform is its ideal. And it's carefully put together by political professionals to put their best foot forward. If you're an outsider, you're invited to like what the party has set forth; if you're already a member, you're invited to support the work of the party. A platform will rarely be implemented in its entirety, but it's supposed to represent what a party would do if it had the power to do anything it wants.

A party's platform is its conscience. This is important to remember, because a platform will tend to guide its politicians back to the party's own path over time. And if the words you read make you nervous, there is good reason. A party in power will try to implement every policy plank it can. Believe it - take them at their word.

A party's platform can be corrupted. Comparing platforms in successive election cycles can be revealing. You can detect the influence of insiders as you observe the continuity of its content. You can also detect the influence of political outsiders and newcomers in the changes you see. Would a border wall have become GOP doctrine in 2016 without the rhetoric of Donald Trump - an outsider? Would criminal justice reform and police reform have been so prominent in the Democratic Party platform without the influence of the Black Lives Matter movement? You may not regard such evolution as corruption, but mainstream party principles are changed over time by such influences, whether for better or worse.

There are exceptions, of course; sometimes parties simply stop in their tracks. The 2016 Republican Party platform was adopted in its entirety, unchanged, for 2020. [1] Because this is the first time it's ever happened, it might be more significant than it seems.

The 2020 Democratic Party platform was influenced not only by the presidential candidate, but also by his closest rival. Together, Joe Biden and Bernie Sanders appointed six commissions to draft policy proposals to be jointly submitted to the Platform Committee. The product of this effort was a 110-page policy recommendation that reflected the positions of both the moderate wing and the progressive wing of the Party.

The contrast between one party's careful development of its platform and the other party's cavalier disregard of its platform is striking. This may reflect the different approach each party takes to achieve unity in its ranks. A party that embraces diversity is bound to craft its platform so that the varied interests of its members are addressed. A party that promotes conformity might simply look to its leader to define its policies as they are implemented.

You'll better understand the political parties by looking at their platforms, and I urge you to read both of them. They are available here…

https://prod-static-ngop-pbl.s3.amazonaws.com/media/documents/DRAFT_12_FINAL[1]-ben_1468872234.pdf

And here…

https://www.google.com/url?sa=t&rct=j&q=&esrc=s&source=web&cd=&ved=2ahUKEwiUn5jl_ajrAhUCba0KHXtlDaQQFjACegQIAxAB&url=https%3A%2F%2Fwww.demconvention.com%2Fwp-content%2Fuploads%2F2020%2F08%2F2020-07-31-Democratic-Party-Platform-For-Distribution.pdf&usg=AOvVaw121154wliveoyTmz4jy5lm

If you'd like to see how they've evolved over the years, the old ones are here...

If you read for comprehension, you'll need a copy of the US Constitution handy. Luckily, it's available here…

Fundamental Party Values

There was a time when the Republican Party had a viable liberal wing and the Democratic Party had a viable conservative wing. Today, this is no longer true. The Republican Party is the champion of conservatism and the Democratic Party is the champion of liberalism. Neither party practices a pure version of its ideology, but each embraces its ideals with vigor. To understand the most fundamental difference between the two parties we must understand the roots and nature of these two political ideologies. Let's look.

Republican - Conservatism

People often define themselves in the best possible light; political parties are no different. The following statements are the Republican Party's description of what it means to be a Party member or supporter. As we proceed through this book together, we can compare and contrast these statements with the platform policies that were set forth in 2016. [2]

"I believe that our:

Country is exceptional

Constitution should be honored, valued, and upheld

Leaders should serve people, not special interests

Families and communities should be strong and free from government intrusion

Institution of traditional marriage is the foundation of society

Government should be smaller, smarter and more efficient

Health care decisions should be made by us and our doctors

Paychecks should not be wasted on poorly run government programs

Military must be strong and prepared to defend our shores

Culture should respect and protect life

Children should never be left in failing schools

Veterans should have the best care and opportunities in the world

Social programs should help lift people out of poverty

America should be energy independent"

Is this a set of conservative values? We live in a new political reality - one in which *conservatism* has become the exclusive standard of the GOP as they jostle for position in the party.

Following on the heels of the Tea Party movement of 2010, GOP leadership - senators, representatives, governors, mayors, and party officials - edged farther and farther to the right. Each one wanted to be the most conservative. The word is still uttered at every opportunity, often in a reverent hush. Conservatives assume that the word carries only positive connotations, and that nobody will pop the hood to see what it really means. But we'll ask the question: *Exactly what does it actually stand for?*

Richard M. Weaver was perhaps the first in the modern era to attempt to create an intellectual framework for conservatism. His *Southern Tradition at Bay* [3], written in 1943, codified the values that would serve the Republican Party well in the 1960s. He identified four southern principles:

Feudalism, in which a family's identity was rooted in its land;

Chivalry, in which a knight's honor derived from medieval tradition;

The gentleman tradition that conferred authority together with obligation; and

Faith, a tradition of subservience to a higher authority.

These principles laid the groundwork for the political shift in the southern states when Lyndon Johnson stood up for civil rights - and for Nixon's *Southern Strategy* that followed. They still serve the interests of the Republican Party today as a foundation to ensure the support of the southern states. In antebellum America, after all, the big-money interests *were* the landed, slaveholding, god-fearing gentry. These principles echo today in the values and rhetoric of white nationalist wing of the GOP.

William F. Buckley, Jr. was perhaps the best known champion of conservatism in the 20th century. He succinctly defines his ideology like this.

> "Conservatism aims to maintain in working order the loyalties of the community to perceived truths and also to those truths which in their judgment have earned universal recognition."

Okay, that's maybe too succinct to mean anything. So let's look at his landmark book, *Up From Liberalism*. [4] Buckley's stated purpose was to bring down liberalism - but why, and what did he mean by liberalism? He viewed it as the most opportunistic ideology of the day, but his view was peculiar. He defined *his* liberal in terms of a straw man who maintains "that the human being is perfectible and social progress predicable" and "...that social and individual differences, if they are not rational, are objectionable, and should be scientifically eliminated." But only half of the book was anti-liberal - the rest advocated economic freedom and small, non-intrusive government. You may recognize these as the building blocks of laissez-faire corporate capitalism.

Perhaps we can learn more about Buckley by checking out his friends and enemies. He embraced Joseph McCarthy and his crusade to rid the country of communists, socialists, and liberals of any stripe. He called Gore Vidal *a queer* on live television - a biting pejorative at the time. And he rejected Ayn Rand - *not for her cruel social Darwinism, but for her atheism.* This inevitably sheds some light on Buckley's conservative principles.

Lewis Powell was another southern champion of conservatism. Powell was a noted attorney who represented the defendants in Brown v. Board of Education and the interests of big tobacco before his confirmation as Nixon's nominee to the Supreme Court. In 1971 he created a plan [5] for the US Chamber of Commerce to extend corporate influence over the institutions of public policy by controlling the content of popular media. His framework - which became known as the *Powell Memorandum* - spawned the Heritage Foundation, American Legislative Exchange Council, the Business Roundtable, and other corporate advocacy organizations.

While the works of Weaver and Buckley were academic and intellectual, Powell's legacy is eminently practical. His prescriptions for controlling media, for purging progressive thought from textbooks, and for vilifying consumerists like Ralph Nader all serve corporatist interests, and are today aggressively pursued nearly fifty years later.

Powell was unique in that he placed the conservative movement in clear opposition to the dearest principles of democratic thought: that the general populace could be manipulated - *ought to be manipulated* - to support corporate interests clearly adverse to their own.

Russell Kirk, via Heritage Foundation, in 1987 penned an essay that provides us the most concise and benign interpretation of conservatism. It was rooted firmly in the soil fertilized by Weaver, Buckley, and Powell. Written during the Reagan years, it was entitled, *Ten Conservative Principles*. [6] They are paraphrased as follows:

> Authoritarianism - Moral truths are permanent and unchanging, and those who stray from them are a threat to order.
>
> Traditionalism - Old customs are what allow society to function peaceably, and any new social order that emerges from defying convention is likely to be inferior.
>
> Anti-modernism - Contemporary thinkers are dwarfs on the shoulders of the thinkers of antiquity, and we are unlikely to make any new discoveries in morals, politics, or taste.
>
> Prudence - We must act only after sufficient reflection and weighing the consequences, and we regard radical liberals as irresponsibly imprudent.
>
> Inequality - The preservation of society requires orders and classes, and egalitarianism in civilization leads to stagnation and tyranny.

Anti-utopian - Because mankind is imperfect no perfect society is possible, and the best we can hope for is a social order in which some evils and suffering are tolerated.

Property - Intergenerational private property ownership is the basis of civilization and freedom, and economic leveling hinders economic progress.

Anti-collectivism - All community must be both voluntary and local, and when community is passed to a centralized authority freedom and human dignity are lost.

Restraint upon power and human passions - People are both good and evil and this requires a balance between authoritarianism and personal liberty.

Anti-progressivism - When a society progresses in one place it declines in another, so it is only the cult of progress that embraces change.

Taken together, the views of Weaver, Buckley, Powell, and Kirk reliably encompass the diversity and define the limits of conservatism as it is practiced and promoted in the 21st century. Diversity can be found in principles that are simultaneously traditionalist, xenophobic, religiously fundamentalist, racist, fiscally responsible, authoritarian, elitist, and libertarian. And the common dogma that defines all strains of conservatism is an anti-modernism that universally regards liberals and progressives with utter disdain.

As a quasi political platform, this aggregation of principles explains the appeal of authoritarian presidential leadership. It explains the overt disdain for views that originate from outside the fraternity of conservatism. It explains - *or at least justifies* - the deification of wealth and the unprecedented concentration of economic and political power. It also shows us that generational inequality is a feature - *not a bug* - in the authoritarian social order perpetuated by conservatives.

A recurring theme in the words and works of conservative thought is the concept of *freedom*. A free society is seen as beneficial, of course, but when we ask, "Freedom for whom?" "Freedom to do what?" or "Freedom *from* what?" today's conservatives rarely provide a concise answer such as:

"/ˈfrēdəm/

> the power or right to act, speak, or think as one wants without hindrance or restraint."

Ironically, freedom is rarely seen in conflict with an authoritarian domestic government or generational inequality. Conservatives rarely use synonyms such as *privilege* or *entitlement*. Instead, they usually point to the US Constitution. Pressed further, they'll direct us to the Second Amendment or the First Amendment - the parts of the latter that deal with speech and religion rather than the parts that deal with assembly and redress. Is America's freedom threatened in 2020? Exactly whose freedom? How is it threatened, and by whom?

~

Democrat - Liberalism / Progressivism

Democrats want to define themselves in the best possible light too. The following statements are the Democratic Party's description of what it stands for. As we proceed through this book together, we can compare and contrast these statements with their 2020 platform policies. [7]

> "Democrats believe health care is a right, diversity is a strength, the economy should work for everyone, and facts and truth matter.
>
> Whether it's health care, the economy, education, gun reform, equal pay, voting rights, national security, or the climate crisis, the Democratic Party understands that there's no single issue that matters more than the rest. Democrats are tackling these issues and others every day."

These statements are much more general than those of the Republican Party. However, the Democratic National Committee will be happy to refer you to the policy planks in its current and prior platforms, with special emphasis on civil rights, education, environment, health care, immigration reform, jobs and the economy, national security, preventing gun violence, retirement security, science and technology, and voting rights.

Does this seem like a set of liberal or progressive values? If it doesn't, it's because the Democratic Party includes not only liberals and progressives, but also political and economic moderates. Even so, if there's an American party that represents liberal values, it's the Democratic Party.

Some care must be taken in defining liberalism. In some dark corners of the American psyche, the term is regarded as a pejorative. Liberals are sometimes painted as radicals, dreamers, and un-American. This is clearly a narrative based on a reactionary position, and for our purposes we'll use a more formal definition. So exactly what is a liberal? The Oxford Dictionary says:

> "adjective
>
> 1. willing to respect or accept behavior or opinions different from one's own; open to new ideas.....
>
> 2. relating to or denoting a political and social philosophy that promotes individual rights, civil liberties, democracy, and free enterprise.....
>
> noun
>
> 1. a supporter of policies that are socially progressive and promote social welfare.
>
> 2. a supporter of a political and social philosophy that promotes individual rights, civil liberties, democracy, and free enterprise....."

Some people draw a sharp distinction between liberalism and progressivism. There's some merit in knowing the differences between liberals and progressives. Historically, the *progressive movement* is associated with a specific period of social activism between about 1890 and 1920. But today's progressives are less concerned with women's suffrage and temperance than they are with the institutions of democracy and racial equality. So it's confusing to cast today's progressives in terms of historical issues.

Instead, we might draw the distinction on the basis of the progressive's belief that the lives of people can be improved by making changes to public policy that correct the mistakes of the past. While liberals may also embrace this belief, they are more associated with specific suites of public policies such as universal health care and a secure retirement for all.

One blogger [8] puts it this way:

> "What Makes Progressive Different From Liberal
>
> Progressives recognize problems and try to define and address the systemic rules, laws and traditions that enable and empower the problems in the first place. Additionally, Progressives share a general belief in the interconnections of individuals and the philosophy that "when you hurt, I hurt".
>
> The Most Important Issue is Money in Politics
>
> The most important issue in most Progressives circles is money in politics - though the climate crisis, social justice and income inequality are pervasive as well. Because money in politics is so influential on our candidates and elected officials, Progressives collectively recognize that our broken campaign finance system affects all issues. Literally, almost no issue goes unaffected by money in politics. Private prisons, gun control, education funding, the climate crisis, the military industrial complex, the over-prescription of pain killers, etc. Very few issues escape the grasp of our oligarchic campaign finance system."

If you know people who identify with one or the other of these labels, you've probably noticed that they agree on many things. So for purposes of this investigation, we'll use *liberal* and *progressive* without further acknowledging the differences between them. The Democratic Party might suggest that we're all on the same team, after all.

The history of liberalism might be longer than you think. While today's conservative movement can be defined by the positions and work of a handful of 20th century intellectuals - Weaver, Buckley, Powell, and Kirk - the roots of liberalism can be traced back to the dawn of civilization. Tracing a zigzag line from Confucius through Pythagoras, Aristotle, Cicero, Aquinas, Descartes, Moore, Bacon, Hobbes, Rousseau, Smith, Kant, de Tocqueville, and many others, we discover one defining characteristic - the progressive's belief that the lives of people can be improved by making changes to public policy - or society as a whole - that correct the mistakes of the past. [9]

Liberals may agree with the conservative belief that our wisdom rests on the shoulders of the giants of political philosophy. But they reject the *unearned deity* of these historical figures and choose instead to carry on their tradition of *questioning the tradition* that's gone before. Liberals, progressives - *and the ancients* - share a willingness to engage the status quo and promote changes to improve it.

A recurring theme in the words and works of liberal thought is the concept of *equality*. An equal society is seen as beneficial. Nelson Mandela paraphrased Mahatma Gandhi when he said, "A Nation should not be judged by how it treats its highest citizens, but its lowest ones."

But equality means different things to different people - and different parties. We often hear the challenge to the goal of equality in the form of a question, "equality of opportunity or equality of outcome?" This challenge is almost always posed by conservatives; after all, if they embrace inequality they can launch the argument, step away, and watch us tear each other apart. But the controversy can illustrate the differences between liberal and progressive approaches.

A liberal approach might be primarily concerned with equality outcomes. Liberals often promote the redistribution of wealth and income as a solution to the undeniable inequalities that have developed in society. This redistribution is usually expressed by policy advocates for welfare and safety-net programs and investment in public goods. Remarkably, these solutions often address the consequences, rather than the causes, of inequality. The liberal approach is to create equality of outcome.

A progressive approach might be primarily concerned with equality of opportunities. Structural, generational inequality is barely addressed by policies of redistribution. If today's liberal policies fail to achieve their desired effect, the progressive has a solution - keep trying new approaches, learning from our mistakes and addressing underlying causes with fundamental, systematic reforms. Because this is a continuing process, it can better focus on the long term rather than immediate results. And fundamental reforms typically require much more time to yield a long-term benefit - the benefit of equal outcomes.

There's a popular myth that equality of opportunity and equality of outcomes are different - but they're actually one and the same. Sure, there are differences among individuals, but such inequalities couldn't persist for a dozen generations without the help of public policy. And there are cultural differences, but the economic variances may reflect the values of the culture rather than an intrinsic, persistent inequality. Are there genetic differences? If you believe there are, you're in the company of social Darwinists and those who blame the poor for their poverty, attributing their fate to their race or some yet-to-be dis-covered gene for poverty itself. That's absurd. And if you think so too, you're forced to accept that - *over time* - equal opportunity afforded to all will erase persistent, structural, generational inequality. That's a good thing - a concept that can unite liberals and progressives.

The Constitution and the Judiciary

We've noted the profound differences between conservative and progressive ideologies, and we've noted how the parties differ in their views of both freedom and equality. These differences drive two very different perspectives on the judiciary and the very constitution upon which it is based. Understanding these perspectives on the nature and purpose of the Constitution can help us understand the platforms.

We need to understand today's two dominant interpretations of the US Constitution - *originalist* and *living*. A little background helps, since some of the biggest differences between Republicans and Democrats can be traced to our attitudes toward the founding documents.

Constitutional Originalism was explicitly embraced in the 2016 Republican Party platform.

> "We affirm - as did the Declaration of Independence: that all are created equal, endowed by their Creator with inalienable rights of life, liberty, and the pursuit of happiness." "We believe the Constitution was written not as a flexible document, but as our enduring covenant." "We affirm that all legislation, regulation, and official actions must conform to the Constitution's original meaning as understood at the time the language was adopted."

Originalism, like conservatism itself, [10] is often accorded a sacred place in the Republican lexicon. Let's take a look at what it means, where it came from, and how it influenced the Republican Party platform. Only then can we make sense of the pseudo-intellectual logic behind the concept by probing some examples.

Paul Brest defines originalism as, "…the familiar approach to constitutional adjudication that accords binding authority to the text of the Constitution or the intentions of its adopters." [11] Brest is a Professor Emeritus at Stanford Law School, and more importantly, he's the guy who coined the term. Breaking it down, he's saying that the law must not only follow the words of the Constitution, it must also conform to what the Framers were thinking.

The Framers themselves didn't give us any such guidance. In fact, originalism wasn't even conjured up until at least 1980 - *yeah, it's that new* - and it didn't rise to its place in right-wing orthodoxy until even more recently. But its gestation took place during 1980s. Originalism - like conservatism, trickle-down economics, and runaway inequality - is America's nightmare legacy of the Reagan years.

Originalism rests on the wobbly foundation of antimodernism - one of the ten pillars of conservatism penned in 1987 by Russell Kirk. If we view America's founders as the very giants to whom Kirk refers, who are we to question their wisdom?

Clearly, originalism and conservatism are close allies. And both have been co-opted by the controlling interests of the Republican Party to promote the agenda of economic concentration and political control. Corporations and the very wealthy - *big-money interests* - have worked hard for centuries to lay down the rules of western economies and governments to serve their own purposes. And they don't want reformers messing up their work; they want to keep things pretty much as they are.

~

What do Democrats have to say about it?

A Living Constitution is implicitly embraced in the 2020 Democratic Party platform.

> "We will appoint U.S. Supreme Court justices and federal judges who look like America, are committed to the rule of law, will uphold individual civil rights and civil liberties as essential components of a free and democratic society, and will respect and enforce foundational precedents, including Brown v. Board of Education and Roe v. Wade. Democrats

are committed to restoring the full power of the Voting Rights Act and ensuring every citizen can access the ballot box."

Although the text may be expressed through the lens of specific issues, the values of a Living Constitution are clearly illustrated. It permits the interpretation of a body of law that evolves over time and adapts to changes in culture, technology, circumstances, and the political realities of a global community - all without being formally amended. It is seen as desirable by liberals, progressive - and of course, by the Democratic Party.

The Founders expected that the future would bring changes in their new nation. Accordingly, and in response to the demands of the states, they provided structures and process for amending the US Constitution. One hundred years ago, nineteen amendments had been ratified. But in the last century, it's become increasingly impractical to propose, pass, and ratify any changes at all. It's more than coincidental that the rise of political parties developed after the constitution was ratified 232 years ago.

Political parties aren't the only change. Buckminster Fuller proposed the *knowledge doubling curve* to illustrate the dynamic that drives change. In the first 100 years of US Constitutional law, human knowledge doubled. Fifty years later, knowledge was doubling every 25 years. How about today?

> "Today things are not as simple as different types of knowledge have different rates of growth. For example, nano-technology knowledge is doubling every two years and clinical knowledge every 18 months. But on average human knowledge is doubling every 13 months. According to IBM, the build out of the "internet of things" will lead to the doubling of knowledge every 12 hours." [12]

The Founders would recognize very little if they were to visit their country today. Transportation, communication, warfare, medicine, commerce, national demographics - all have transformed today's world beyond the recognition of Washington, Hamilton, and Jefferson. As wise as they were in their day, they would not expect their 21st century country to be governed by literal 18th century laws and standards.

In 2003, Supreme Court Justice Stephen Breyer said on ABC News This Week with George Stephanopolus, in support of a living constitution:

> "Through commerce, through globalization, through the spread of democratic institutions, through immigration to America, it's becoming more and more one world of many different kinds of people. And how they're going to live together across the world will be the challenge, and whether our Constitution and how it fits into the governing documents of other nations, I think will be a challenge for the next generation." [13]

Those who embrace a living constitution understand the threat of constitutional originalism and the threat of conservatism in general. By blocking changes in law that are required to respond to real changes in the country and the world, conservatives are *locking in* the structures and processes they have co-opted over the centuries. Constitutional originalism is the friend of those who are committed to holding on to their power; a living constitution is the friend of those who challenge inequities.

Why is it important to consider fundamental legal frameworks while we're comparing political platforms? Political parties directly control the makeup of both the legislative branch and the executive branch of the US government. Less directly, political parties also control the makeup of the judicial branch as well. Federal judges are known by their records on civil rights, corporate personhood, campaign finance, capital punishment, abortion, voting rights, and an array of other issues featured in party platforms. The party in power has a degree of authority to influence the political complexion of the courts of the land. For example, of 870 federal judges, more than 200 were nominated by the incumbent President and confirmed by the Republican Senate. The litmus test for each of these was adherence to the ideology of constitutional originalism.

Political Power and Values

Politics is all about power. And if there's a fundamental value that each party holds in common with the other, it's the acquisition and perpetuation of its own power. Of course, this is a zero-sum game in which one party's power can only be increased at the relative expense of the other party. But discussions of power - *beating the other party* - in the context of party platforms are largely absent. Strategies and tactics for beating the other party are developed and implemented in campaigns rather than in policy platforms.

At times the acquisition and perpetuation of power comes in conflict with other fundamental party values - and the power grab often wins. Democrats take corporate money, fully knowing that it will undermine their platform. Republicans follow a leader quick to violate conservative principles to promote his personal agenda. So do not assume that the values of a party will always drive its policies; political parties, like people, sometimes stray from their principles to get what they want.

BASIC VALUES

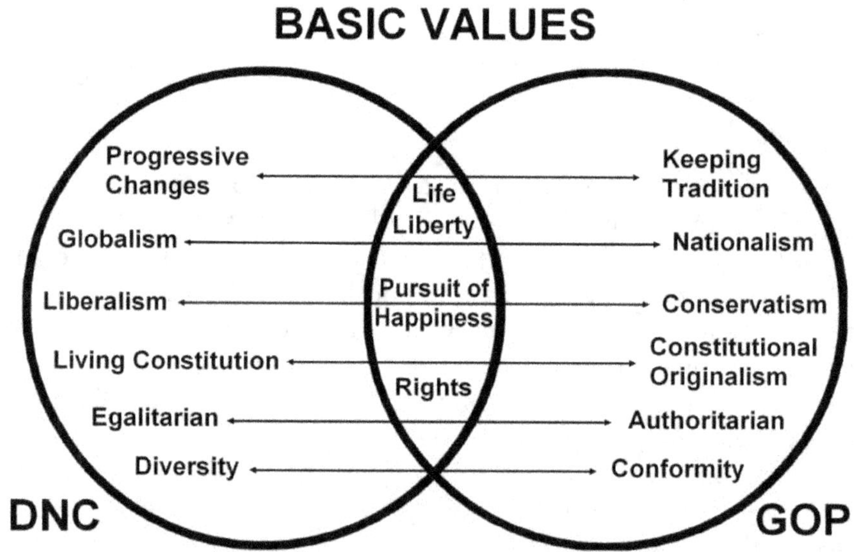

There really is a difference between the parties. Their most fundamental values are rooted in different places, times, and social positions. And while the parties agree that Americans may rightly lay claim to life, liberty, and the pursuit of happiness, they diverge in defining the beliefs and approaches needed to fulfill the claims.

[1] https://www.vanityfair.com/news/2020/06/republican-party-keeping-2016-platform-2020

[2] https://www.gop.com/platform/

[3] https://www.kirkusreviews.com/book-reviews/a/richard-weaver/the-southern-tradition-at-bay/

[4] https://www.ebooks-library.com/author.cfm/AuthorID/2125

[5] https://reclaimdemocracy.org/powell_memo_lewis/

[6] https://kirkcenter.org/conservatism/ten-conservative-principles/

[7] https://democrats.org/where-we-stand/

[8] https://the2020progressive.com/difference-liberal-progressive/

[9] https://www.theatlantic.com/politics/archive/2014/02/the-origin-of-liberalism/283780/

[10] http://www.opednews.com/articles/The-Threat-of-Conservatism-by-Larry-Butler-Antiquity_Authoritarianism_Bigotry_Buckley-160227-532.html

[11] http://scholarship.law.georgetown.edu/cgi/viewcontent.cgi?article=2362&context=facpub

[12] https://www.industrytap.com/knowledge-doubling-every-12-months-soon-to-be-every-12-hours/3950

[13] https://ballotpedia.org/Living_Constitution

LIES

Where's the Focus

Many voters make their choices on the basis of the candidate - his or her charisma, experience in or out of office, or ability to stir a crowd. A party's platform may reflect the personality and priorities of its candidate, but it goes much deeper into the values and priorities of the party itself. A party's values and priorities shape the policies it promotes.

So policy matters, and reading the respective platforms of the Democratic and Republican parties can be pretty interesting. You may have heard a popular narrative: *There's no real difference between the parties; they're both corrupt, ignorant of the real needs of the people.* Yes, similarities in structure, function, and funding can certainly be found, in part because they operate in the same environment. Common legal, technological, cultural, and historical structures and processes define and constrain how parties can function. But we'll examine the narrative and expose it for what it is - simply a popular myth propagated by those who, for their own purposes, want you to believe it. On the following pages you'll find a consistent theme: there are deep and stark differences between the two parties that we need to understand.

That said, let's start with the general stuff. To identify priorities of focus, look at the result of key-word searches on each of the two platforms. Here is a sampling, arranged in order of the frequency of mentions in the GOP platform.

The View from the Right

Key Word	Mentions	
"Republican"	GOP - 144	Democrat - 18
"Regulation"	GOP - 82	Democrat - 4
"Military "	GOP - 55	Democrat - 44
"Democrat"	GOP - 53	Democrat - 466
"Economy"	GOP - 53	Democrat - 59
"Energy"	GOP - 48	6 Democrat - 0

"Freedom"	GOP - 45	Democrat - 14
"Great"	GOP - 43	Democrat - 34
"Growth"	GOP - 40	Democrat - 6
"Limit"	GOP - 38	Democrat - 5
"Environment"	GOP - 37	Democrat - 29
"Jobs"	GOP - 32	Democrat - 58
"Trade"	GOP - 31	Democrat - 19
"Women"	GOP - 28	Democrat - 64
"Terror"	GOP - 26	Democrat - 18
"Obama"	GOP - 20	Democrat - 16
"God"	GOP - 16	Democrat - 1
"Poverty"	GOP - 15	Democrat - 16
"Reagan"	GOP - 11	Democrat - 0
"Election / Electoral"	GOP - 10	Democrat - 16
"Russia / Russian"	GOP - 10	Democrat - 5
"Christian"	GOP - 8	Democrat - 1
"Climate change"	GOP - 7	Democrat - 24
"Corrupt / Corruption"	GOP - 7	Democrat - 11
"Biden"	GOP - 5	Democrat - 16
"Muslim"	GOP - 4	Democrat - 4
"Persecution"	GOP - 4	Democrat - 2
"Corporations "	GOP - 3	Democrat - 18
"Police"	GOP - 3	Democrat - 13
"Conservative"	GOP - 3	Democrat - 0
"Impeach"	GOP - 2	Democrat - 0
"Law and Order"	GOP - 2	Democrat - 0
"Trump "	GOP - 0	Democrat - 114
"Pandemic"	GOP - 0	Democrat - 75
"Covid / coronavirus"	GOP - 0	Democrat - 59

"Equality / Equity "	GOP - 0	Democrat - 22
"Lives Matter"	GOP - 0	Democrat - 2
"Fascist"	GOP - 0	Democrat - 1

~

The View from the Left

Here is the same list, in order of the frequency of mentions in the Democratic platform.

Key Word	Mentions	
"Democrat"	GOP - 53	Democrat - 466
"Trump "	GOP - 0	Democrat - 114
"Pandemic"	GOP - 0	Democrat - 75
"Women"	GOP - 28	Democrat - 64
"Energy"	GOP - 48	Democrat - 60
"Economy"	GOP - 53	Democrat - 59
"Covid / coronavirus"	GOP - 0	Democrat - 59
"Jobs"	GOP - 32	Democrat - 58
"Military "	GOP - 55	Democrat - 44
"Great"	GOP - 43	Democrat - 34
"Environment"	GOP - 37	Democrat - 29
"Climate change"	GOP - 7	Democrat - 24
"Equality / Equity "	GOP - 0	Democrat - 22
"Trade"	GOP - 31	Democrat - 19
"Republican"	GOP - 144	Democrat - 18
"Terror"	GOP - 26	Democrat - 18
"Corporations "	GOP - 3	Democrat - 18
"Obama"	GOP - 20	Democrat - 16
"Poverty"	GOP - 15	Democrat - 16
"Election / Electoral"	GOP - 10	Democrat - 16
"Biden"	GOP - 5	Democrat - 16

"Freedom"	GOP - 45	Democrat - 14
"Police"	GOP - 3	Democrat - 13
"Corrupt / Corruption"	GOP - 7	Democrat - 11
"Growth"	GOP - 40	Democrat - 6
"Limit"	GOP - 38	Democrat - 5
"Russia / Russian"	GOP - 10	Democrat - 5
"Regulation"	GOP - 82	Democrat - 4
"Muslim"	GOP - 4	Democrat - 4
"Persecution"	GOP - 4	Democrat - 2
"Lives Matter"	GOP - 0	Democrat - 2
"God"	GOP - 16	Democrat - 1
"Christian"	GOP - 8	Democrat - 1
"Fascist"	GOP - 0	Democrat - 1
"Reagan"	GOP - 11	Democrat - 0
"Conservative"	GOP - 3	Democrat - 0
"Impeach"	GOP - 2	Democrat - 0
"Law and Order"	GOP - 2	Democrat - 0

This can certainly inform us on the focus on issues, but not the position itself. The Republican platform, for example, cited "climate change" 7 times, but *every one* of the citations referred to positions *opposed* by the party. Likewise, while the Democratic platform referred 114 times to "Trump," no support for the candidate is indicated.

Even so, the list shows priorities of focus. Both parties like to talk about themselves, and the frequency of their own name is right at the top of their lists. Republicans like to talk about the military and the other party, while Democrats like to talk about jobs, women, and Trump - the latter a subject discreetly avoided by the GOP platform!

The party of the incumbent administration can be expected to focus on what it will do to promote existing agendas. This makes the use of the 2016 platform by the GOP all the more perplexing. To an extreme degree, the provisions set forth four years ago have been implemented. Corporate tax cuts, deregulation, and curtailing immigration are a *fait accompli*. There is some unfinished business, of course; Obamacare has yet to be fully dismantled. But the perceived ills and transgressions of the preceding administration are simply irrelevant in 2020.

To this end, Democrats focus more detailed policy positions on regulation, inequality, civil rights, spending initiatives, and universal health care. By contrast, the GOP focused more on what it would undo in order to reverse the evils wrought by the [prior] administration, unconcerned over the obvious reversals that have been wrought by the new incumbent. To this end, Republicans were specific in their positions regarding Obamacare, green energy initiatives, and the diplomatic policies of previous administrations, promising in each case to reverse direction. And the Republican policy framework was much more general, perhaps deferring to its candidate - even back in 2016 - to flesh out the details using the platform as a guideline.

Read the platforms for yourself and understand how their positions define what and who each of the parties stands for. The worldviews reflected in the platforms illustrate the enormous differences between Republicans and Democrats. Each party promotes the interests and protects the rights of a different constituency. To the degree that a platform proves an honest and genuine guide to public policy proposals, we can determine for ourselves if *our own* values and interests are fairly represented by *our own* party.

Yes, Virginia, there really is a difference.

LIES

The Elephants in the Room

A party's platform typically sets forth fundamental values and goals and policy proposals regarding ongoing critical issues such as climate change, population growth and mobility, and economic inequality; and such existential threats can't be minimized. But a platform also deals with current issues that require a public policy response. A platform recycled from four years earlier may adequately deal with the fundamentals, but it necessarily ignores any current issues, large or small, that have arisen during the current cycle. These are the elephants in the room; some of them are busting up the furniture and defecating on the carpet.

Covid-19 Pandemic

An ongoing severe public health crisis is a defining difference between the platforms of the parties. A platform written before the Covid-19 pandemic falls woefully short in policy solutions. But the response of the incumbent Republican administration gives us some idea of what policies might be implemented in the future. Here is an abbreviated timeline.

In May, 2018 the administration disbanded the White House pandemic response team. In July, 2019, the CDC epidemiology post to China's disease control agency was eliminated.

In January, 2020 the President claimed to have the virus under control, praised China's handling of it, then restricted direct travel from the Chinese mainland. During February, the President assured the nation that the problem was going away.

During March, the administration made false and conflicting claims about testing, contagion, the origin of the virus, personal protective equipment, and ventilators. Four different administration officials were placed in charge of the single task of mobilizing a logistical response, even while claiming that there was no impending public health issue. Then he banned travel from Europe. A $2 trillion relief package was signed into law. Daily case counts increased exponentially. The US death toll rose to 5,000.

In April, the administration largely passed the strategy response to the states, even while attacking Democratic governors. FEMA and the Corps of Engineers began to deploy emergency facilities. The President promoted the use of hydroxychloroquine and disinfectant injections as a cure and claimed that the pandemic would just go away. Nearly $500 billion in business relief was signed into law. The US death toll rose to 65,000.

In May, 38 million jobless claims heralded a looming economic crisis. The administration touted its success in dealing with the pandemic and its support for the deployment of testing resources and vaccine development. The President announced the termination of America's relationship with the World Health Organization. The US death toll rose to 108,000.

In June, the President falsely claimed that China was to blame for the virus, that the pandemic would just disappear, that vaccines would be available within a few months, that the US economy was roaring back, and that expanded testing was the root cause of increase case counts. As case counts rose, death counts declined. The US death toll rose to 130,000.

In July, the President and the CDC came into conflict with regard to the opening of schools. The administration falsely claimed that the US response compared favorably with that of other nations, and that "fake news" was to blame. The responsibility for data collection and reporting was removed from the CDC and awarded to *TeleTracking* - an untested private contractor selected by the administration. The quality of the data has since been described by public health officials as a "hot mess." Even so, as case counts began to moderate, death counts resurged. The US death toll rose to 156,000. [1]

The complete and total absence of any guiding principles or policy planks in the above timeline is stunning. And although the Republican Party remains mute on the values, principles, and policies that might guide an administration in its second term, it continues to call for cutbacks. Medicare and Medicaid were clearly in the crosshairs of GOP spending hawks four years ago, and remain so today. Although both programs have served their participants well during the Covid-19 pandemic, the Party continues to call for limiting, rather than expanding, Medicare eligibility. Calls continue for Medicaid to be removed from federal jurisdiction, given to states, and funded by block grants.

~

The Democratic Party platform deals prominently and explicitly with the pandemic. Here's what the Party would do.

> "We must start by making COVID-19 testing widely available, convenient, and free to everyone."

> "Democrats support making COVID-19 testing, treatment, and any eventual vaccines free to everyone, regardless of their wealth, insurance coverage, or immigration status. We are all only as safe from this disease as are the most vulnerable among us."

> "Democrats will act swiftly to stand up a comprehensive, national public health surveillance program for COVID-19 and future infectious diseases."

> "We will substantially increase funding for the Centers for Disease Control and Prevention (CDC) and for state and local public health departments....."

> "We will provide funding to stabilize the [education] sector and ensure child care and educational settings are able to meet the highest possible public health and worker safety standards to protect the health of care workers, children, parents, and the broader community."

> "We will immediately enact robust paid sick leave protections as part of the COVID-19 response for all workers in the economy, including contractors, gig workers, domestic workers, and the self-employed."

> "Democrats will support funding [to Native American health institutions] to hire sufficient staff to conduct contact tracing for all who test positive for this deadly disease."

The Democratic Party promises action based on the implicit recognition that the US faces a serious and ongoing public health crisis that has been poorly addressed. Each action is accompanied by commensurate added - but unspecified - spending.

Russian Election Attacks

The GOP was mute on the subject of Russian attacks on the general election of 2016, despite the fact that many of the campaign operatives and party officials were directly involved. If we wouldn't expect to see the subject raised in the 2016 GOP platform, we certainly wouldn't expect to see it acknowledged in the current cycle.

Party officials and spokespeople have weighed in on the matter during the incumbent Republican administration with both words and actions. Most notably, the President fired FBI chief James Comey for his investigation of Russian interference. The subsequent report by Special Counsel Robert Mueller revealed numerous connections between Russian operatives and the Trump campaign. None of these connections were regarded as sufficient for criminal prosecution, in part because of the administration's consistent refusal to allow access to testimony and evidence. Several of the instances of obstruction of justice - many of which *were* worthy of prosecution - were related to hiding evidence or testimony about cooperation, coordination, or conspiracy with Russian entities or persons. [2]

In recent years, Senate Majority Leader McConnell has repeatedly blocked the consideration of numerous election security bills crafted to protect the institution against foreign attacks. Notably, Robert Mueller himself raised the alarm in May, 2019: "I will close by reiterating the central allegation of our indictments - that there were multiple, systematic efforts to interfere in our election. That allegation deserves the attention of every American." [3]

If the acts of the GOP served to keep the door open for future Russian attacks, the words of the President were even more explicit. He repeatedly referred to the Special Counsel investigation as a "hoax." After the Mueller Report was submitted to Trump's Attorney General, but before any part of the report was made public, the President said, "After three years of lies and smears and slander, the Russia hoax is finally dead. The collusion delusion is over,"

But the threat remains.

~

We might understand when the Republican Party looks the other way when foreign entities interfere on its behalf. But Russian interference in US elections is real and continuing - as confirmed by our own intelligence community. What does the Democratic Party have to say?

> "We will not tolerate election interference and will protect the integrity of our elections from all enemies, foreign and domestic."

> "Democrats will work with Congress on legislation to... crack down on foreign nationals who try to influence elections..."

> "Democrats will increase investments to help state and local governments upgrade election technology, including cybersecurity technology, and ensure that election technology is accessible for people with disabilities. We will not tolerate election interference and will protect the integrity of our elections from all enemies, foreign and domestic."

> "We expect technology companies and social media platforms to take responsibility and do more to identify foreign disinformation and preserve the openness of democratic societies, and we will take steps to prevent the use of new technologies to facilitate repression, spread hate, or incite violence."

These measures are weak. They are general. And they are accompanied by none of the outrage expected by an attack by a foreign state. And yet the attacks were described as *an act of war* by public figures ranging from Dick Cheney to Nikki Haley to Representative Steve Cohen to Madeleine Albright to Condoleezza Rice to Richard Clarke.

Why the tepid Democratic stance? Is it possible that the Party has surrendered control of the narrative to the President? Has he won the battle of words by repeating *Russia hoax* ad infinitum?

Black Lives and Civil Unrest

Police brutality and racially motivated violence have infected American history for centuries. The positions of Republicans and Democrats can be seen in stark contrast. Following the killing of

George Floyd by Minneapolis police officers, civil unrest spread throughout the country. Demonstrations rallied around the values defined by Black Lives Matter, and there were instances of property destruction and looting.

The 2016 Republican platform offered this guidance.

> "...the next president must not sow seeds of division and distrust between the police and the people they have sworn to serve and protect. The Republican Party, a party of law and order, must make clear in words and action that every human life matters."

In this statement we can detect at least two *dog whistles* - carefully aimed political messages intended for a particular group. To many Americans, *Law and order* simply means respect for the law and obedience to authority; but Richard Nixon recast it to mean increased policing of black communities to keep them under control. Nixon's reframing has been reprised in GOP platforms and values ever since - and has enjoyed a resurgence in Trump's authoritarian-racist rhetoric.

The statement within this context that "every human life matters" is a concession to the white supremacist chant, *all lives matter!* It further repudiates the values and goals of Black Lives Matter, and denies the reality of police brutality - and even the underlying causes of the civil unrest that had long been a part of America's cultural landscape.

The Party's guidance was followed by the incumbent Republican Administration. Incendiary public statements regarding the treatment of detainees by law enforcement, while not explicitly racist, carried a stochastic message of violence. "Please don't be too nice..... Like when you guys put somebody in the car and you're protecting their head, you know, the way you put your hand over it. Like, don't hit their head, and they've just killed somebody... you can take the hand away, O.K.?"

An authoritarian position against protests was maintained throughout the administration. If police violence was a problem, more police violence was seen as the solution. The deployment of federal militarized law enforcement officers in Washington DC and Portland, Oregon put teeth into the threat to occupy the streets of other cities that had elected Democratic leaders.

Democrats take a much wider view of racial injustice and criminal law enforcement. They recognize that both civil unrest and police violence are consequences of societal divisions. And they have a lot to say about the issue.

> "Democrats will root out structural and systemic racism in our economy and our society, and reform our criminal justice system from top to bottom, because we believe Black lives matter."

> "Democrats believe we need to overhaul the criminal justice system from top to bottom. Police brutality is a stain on the soul of our nation."

> "We believe Black lives matter, and will establish a national commission to examine the lasting economic effects of slavery, Jim Crow segregation, and racially discriminatory federal policies on income, wealth, educational, health, and employment outcomes; to pursue truth and promote racial healing; and to study reparations"

> "It is unacceptable that more than 1,000 people, a quarter of them Black, have been killed by police every year since 2015.

> "Democrats will reinvigorate pattern-or-practice investigations into police misconduct at the Department of Justice, and strengthen them through new subpoena powers and expanded oversight to address systemic misconduct by prosecutors."

> "Democrats also support measures to increase diversity among the ranks of police departments, so our law enforcement agencies look more like the communities they serve."

While Democrats may not have all of the public policy solutions, they recognize the broader parameters of the problem. And they reject the notion that civil unrest must be met with force.

Family Separation

Immigration and border security issues are nothing new to American politics. Until recently, little was said and less was known about the separation of children from parents at the southern border. Prior administrations separated children from some parents who were referred for criminal prosecution; throwing kids into jail with mom or dad was never a good policy. During the Obama administration, nearly 500,000 border apprehensions were referred for prosecution, but the number of children involved is unknown. [4]

The international community regards the separation of families to be a violation of law. Ravina Shamdasani, a spokeswoman for the Office of the United Nations High Commissioner for Human Rights said, "[Family separation] amounts to arbitrary and unlawful interference in family life, and is a serious violation of the rights of the child....." [5]

The Republican Party platform had nothing to say about family separation in 2016, but it offered implicit guidance that seemed to favor a hard line against illegal immigrants and refuge seekers.

> "…border security is a national security issue, and that our nation's immigration and refugee policies are placing Americans at risk."

> "We oppose any form of amnesty for those who, by breaking the law, have disadvantaged those who have obeyed it."

The President went well beyond the guidance of his party's platform. Immigration, refugee, and asylum quotas were reduced to levels not seen in decades, and vigorous enforcement of border security confronted those desperate enough to seek entry illegally. While the separation of children from parents had been incidental to the normal processes of arrest and incarceration in prior administrations, the separation itself had never been seen as a strategy. [6] Beginning in mid-2017 all adults, without exception, who crossed without permission near El Paso were detained and criminally charged. Children were taken from them without any provision for tracking and reuniting them. By the end of the year, this policy had been rolled out all along the border.

The following June, the Department of Justice formally announced the policy and called it *zero tolerance*. The DOJ admitted to separating some 2,000 children from parents and placing them in for-profit detention centers. The public outcry was met with an executive order prohibiting family separations *except under various circumstances* and claims that the blame lay with Congress, not the administration. The

President claimed, without evidence, that separating families at the border serves as a deterrent to immigration. [7]

Separations continue as de facto policy, in defiance of an executive order that was barely acknowledged and rarely enforced.

~

The Democratic Party, along with the vast majority of Americans and the International community, stands against the practice and policy of separating families.

> "This Administration's cruelty and dehumanization of immigrants stretches the imagination and shocks the conscience: forcibly separating families and putting children in cages....."

> "Democrats believe that our fight to end systemic and structural racism in our country extends to our immigration system, including the policies at our borders and ports of entry, detention centers, and within immigration law enforcement agencies and their policies and operations."

> "Democrats believe family unity should be a guiding principle for our immigration policy. We will prioritize family reunification for children still separated from their families, and we will restore family reunification programs ended by the Trump Administration."

> "We will end for-profit detention centers and ensure that any facility where migrants are being detained is held to the highest standards of care and guarantees their safety and dignity. Detention of children should be restricted to the shortest possible time, with their access to education and proper care ensured."

> "We will demand that leaders of our immigration agencies be Senate-confirmed professionals, and that Immigration and Customs Enforcement and Customs and Border Protection personnel abide by our values and professional, evidence-based standards and are held accountable for any inappropriate, unlawful, or inhumane treatment."

The egregious trampling of human rights in the name of the United States disturbs and conscience and troubles the soul. Republicans' silence on family separation and other issues that have arisen since their 2016 platform is understandable; they're simply too cowardly to acknowledge the gross injustices in which they are complicit.

[1] https://doggett.house.gov/media-center/blog-posts/timeline-trump-s-coronavirus-responses

[2] https://www.cnn.com/2019/04/18/politics/full-mueller-report-pdf/index.html

[3] https://www.salon.com/2019/05/30/despite-muellers-warning-mcconnell-blocks-bipartisan-election-security-bills/

[4] https://www.factcheck.org/2018/06/did-the-obama-administration-separate-families/

[5] https://www.nytimes.com/2018/06/05/world/americas/us-un-migrant-children-families.html

[6] https://www.splcenter.org/news/2020/06/17/family-separation-under-trump-administration-timeline

[7] https://apnews.com/2fd81e62756b4624a5ddc86acca8a19e

Equality and Freedom

Make no mistake - there is a difference between the policy platforms of Republicans and Democrats. Virtually every public policy has an impact on economic and social equality, and many public policies have an impact on our degree of perceived and actual equality and freedom.

Republicans generally regard equality and freedom to be exclusive from each other. Seen on a linear scale, each is at the opposite extreme. This notion is often justified by drawing a contrast between *free* societies and *socialist* societies. Free societies are assumed to be purely capitalist societies and socialist societies are assumed to be uniformly regulated economies. Using these assumptions, they observe, correctly or incorrectly, that free societies are inherently unequal while socialist societies are inherently equal. One writer puts it like this:

> "If you look at relatively free societies, like democracies, you'll see tremendous amount of inequality exist. In the United States, the hot issue now is income inequality. Similarly, there are inequalities in terms of social influence and political power. These inequalities exist in free societies because they allow the natural inequalities of humans to compound. In other words, left unchecked or free, the natural state of humanity is inequality. Similarly, if you look at relatively less free societies, like ones based on socialism or communism, you will see that the people are much more equal. Most people living in socialist or communist countries are around the same socioeconomic status. While there may be more equality, the people in these societies have much less individual freedom. There is a tradeoff between equality and freedom." [1]

Democrats - liberals and progressives - are more nuanced in their view of the juxtaposition of equality and freedom. They recognize a relatedness rather than a dichotomy between the two concepts. And they ask, "Freedom for whom?" and "what kind of freedom?" and even "what kind of equality?"

"Freedom is a value worth fighting for, but so is Equality; and
I would argue that there is no need to make a choice between
the two, as you cannot have one without the other. True Freedom requires true Equality. While social, economic and political hierarchies exist, both freedom and equality cannot exist.
To quote Mikhail Bakunin, "political freedom without economic equality is a pretense, a fraud, a lie". The root of all un-
freedom is authority; vertical power structures necessarily
restrict the freedom of the weaker party by virtue of where
power lies in the relationship between the two." [2]

Equality

Not everybody agrees that equality is an issue. The word "inequality"
fails to make an appearance anywhere in the GOP platform, and the
word "equality" appears only twice. After all, one of the fundamentals
of conservatism is that generational inequality is the basis of western
civilization - starting with the very concept of *American exceptionalism.*

"The Declaration sets forth the fundamental precepts of
American government: That God bestows certain inalienable
rights on every individual, thus producing human equality; that
government exists first and foremost to protect those inalienable rights; that man-made law must be consistent with God-
given, natural rights....."

"We continue to encourage equality for all citizens and access
to the American Dream. Merit and hard work should determine advancement in our society, so we reject unfair preferences, quotas, and set-asides as forms of discrimination."

Clearly, neither of these statements specifies public policies embraced
or to be implemented by the party. Instead, they are general statements of principle; the former leaves equality to God and the latter
carries an explicit rejection of specific policies that address inequality.

~

In stark contrast, the words "equality," "inequality," and "equity"
appear 22 times in the Democratic Party platform. It leaves no doubt
as to the Party's values and principles.

"Democrats stand ready to take immediate, decisive action to pull the economy out of President Trump's recession by... enacting fundamental reforms to address structural and systemic racism and entrenched income and wealth inequality in our economy and our banking system."

"We will direct federal regulators to review a subset of the mergers and acquisitions that have taken place since President Trump took office... to assess whether any have increased market concentration, raised consumer prices, demonstrably harmed workers, increased racial inequality, reduced competition, or constricted innovation, and assign appropriate remedies."

"We will take aggressive action to end pay inequality, including by increasing penalties against companies that discriminate against women and passing the Paycheck Fairness Act."

"We will enhance our coordination and joint standard setting [with European countries] on technology, trade, and investment, and we will work to boost our post-COVID-19 economic recovery and reduce inequality."

"Democrats will fight to guarantee equal rights for women, including by ratifying the Equal Rights Amendment and at long last enshrining gender equality in the U.S. Constitution"

"We will fight to enact the Equality Act and at last outlaw discrimination against LGBTQ+ people....."

"Democrats believe we can and must do better for our children, our educators, and our country.

"We are committed to making the investments our students and teachers need to build equity and safeguard humanity in our educational system and guarantee every child can receive a great education."

Freedom

How is freedom an issue today? The words "freedom" and "free" appeared 45 times and 40 times, respectively, in the GOP Platform.

Freedoms come in a variety of flavors and styles, and they're some-times confused with rights. It's enlightening to recognize the distinction between the two: [3]

> "A Right is a common privilege given to all citizens for example the right to vote, the right to property, the right to worship, the right to information, etc. Freedom is when you have no constraints to [the conduct of] your actions."

Notably, the US Constitution uses the word freedom only in reference to "...speech, or of the press, or the *right* of the people peaceably to assemble, and to petition the Government for a redress of grievances." (Italics added for emphasis.)

The GOP platform referred to a variety of freedoms and rights mostly as *freedoms*. The greatest number of mentions - eighteen in all - by far referred to economic or property freedom.

> "We believe political freedom and economic freedom are indivisible."

> "When political freedom and economic freedom are separated - both are in peril; when united, they are invincible."

> "We are the party of a growing economy that gives everyone a chance in life, an opportunity to learn, work, and realize the prosperity freedom makes possible."

> "Government must give America's innovators the freedom to create and, on their merits, succeed or fail."

> "We pledge to be the best partner of all African nations in their pursuit of economic freedom and human rights."

Other mentions of freedom in the GOP platform *indirectly* impact economic freedom -for example,

> "The rights of citizenship do not stop at the ballot box. Freedom of speech includes the right to devote resources to whatever cause or candidate one supports."

Although this clause promoted the principle of money as political speech, speech itself isn't the point; *it was about the money,* and what it can do.

That raises the question of *exactly who* is to enjoy economic freedom. Republicans respected the collective when the collective is a business corporation, and generally failed to distinguish between collective corporate freedom and individual freedom.

> "We support repeal of federal restrictions on political parties in McCain-Feingold, raising or repealing contribution limits, protecting the political speech of advocacy groups, corporations, and labor unions, and protecting political speech on the internet."

The GOP platform also referred frequently to freedom of religion - eleven times in all.

> "Religious freedom in the Bill of Rights protects the right of the people to practice their faith in their everyday lives."

> "We support repeal of the Johnson Amendment, which restricts First Amendment freedoms of all nonprofit organizations by prohibiting political speech."

> "A Republican commander-in-chief will protect the religious freedom of all military members, especially chaplains, and will not tolerate attempts to ban Bibles or religious symbols from military facilities." [4]

Freedom - especially of religion - was even a prominent feature of the *foreign policy planks* of the GOP platform.

> "...a Republican administration will return the advocacy of religious liberty to a central place in its diplomacy....."

> "The U.S. Commission on International Religious Freedom, an initiative of Congressional Republicans, has been neglected by the current [prior] Administration at a time when its voice more than ever needs to be heard."

> "Israel is likewise an exceptional country that shares our most essential values. It is the only country in the Middle East where freedom of speech and freedom of religion are found."

> "We cannot overlook the continued repression of fundamental rights and religious freedom [In Vietnam], as well as retribution against ethnic minorities and others who assisted U.S. forces during the conflict there.

> "The United States must stand with leaders, like President Sisi
> of Egypt who has bravely protected the rights of Coptic
> Christians in Egypt....."

For those who had read and understood the 2016 GOP platform, it
came as no surprise when Secretary of State Pompeo declared property rights and religious liberty to be paramount. "It's important for
every American, and for every American diplomat, to recognize how
our founders understood unalienable rights. Foremost among these
rights are property rights and religious liberty." [5]

For those who value conventional human rights and liberties - equality,
freedom from discrimination, the right to life, liberty, and personal security, freedom from slavery, and even freedom from torture -
Pompeo's statement was shocking in its callous ignorance.

~

What does the Democratic Party platform have to say about freedom?
The words, "freedom" and "free" appear 12 times and 22 times, respectively. Six of the appearances referenced the price of goods or
services such as vaccines or education. What about the rest - do
Democrats share an understanding with Republicans of the nature of
freedom?

Economic freedom, including property freedom, commanded a
prominent place in the 2016 GOP platform. Remarkably, the
Democratic Party platform makes not a single reference to the context
of economic freedom or property rights.

Religious freedom, in principle, is a shared value of the two parties.

> "Democrats believe that freedom of religion is a fundamental
> human right....."

> "And we will ban racial and religious profiling in law
> enforcement."

> "We will reject the Trump Administration's use of broad
> religious exemptions to allow businesses, medical providers,
> social service agencies, and others to discriminate."

> "We will confront white nationalist terrorism and combat hate
> crimes perpetrated against religious minorities."

Democrats are clear in their defense of freedom of speech and freedom of the press.

"The free press is essential to our free democracy."

"Independent media is not the enemy of the people, but the guardian of democracy."

"We will push back against erosion of press freedom wherever it occurs and in whatever form - whether through direct intimidation of, and violence against, journalists or legal, regulatory, and financial pressures that smother free speech."

Democrats defend the intellectual freedom of America's scientists and academics.

"Democrats will protect the independence and intellectual freedom of scientists, whether they are employed by the federal government or receiving federal grants in support of their research, and take steps to shield our scientific research agencies from future political interference."

"And Democrats will safeguard academic freedom on college campuses."

Democrats also view freedom as a driving value in US foreign policy.

"We will reverse the Trump Administration's politicization of religious freedom in American foreign policy....."

"We oppose any effort to unfairly single out and delegitimize Israel... through the Boycott, Divestment, and Sanctions Movement, while protecting the Constitutional right of our citizens to free speech."

Republicans and Democrats agree in principle on freedom of religion, but the policies and practices of the parties diverge. And while Republicans value economic, property - and corporate - freedoms, Democrats value intellectual freedom, freedom of speech, and freedom of the press.

Do freedom and equality interrelate, or are they simply points at the end of a continuum? Long ago I met an old freedom rider, active in the early days of the modern civil rights movement. His words, few as they were, stayed with me over the years. He said...

If degrees of freedom available to us are different, we're not equal. If opportunities are more available to some than they are to others, we're not equal. If we're not equal, we're not free. And we're not free 'til we're *all* free!

Taxes, Spending, Equality, and Freedom

GOP budget and tax proposals - contained in the 2016 platform and partially implemented during the incumbent administration - promoted tax cuts, increased spending on defense and security, and reduced spending elsewhere. And these proposals came directly from the platform.

> "As Republicans, we oppose tax increases and believe in the power of markets to create wealth and to help secure the future of our Social Security system."

> "To preserve Medicare and Medicaid, the financing of these important programs must be brought under control before they consume most of the federal budget, including national defense."

> "[re Medicare] Without disadvantaging present retirees or those nearing retirement, set a more realistic age for eligibility in light of today's longer life span."

> "We applaud the Republican governors and state legislators who have undertaken the hard work of modernizing Medicaid. We will give them a free hand to do so by block-granting the program without strings."

> "The Republican path to fiscal sanity and economic expansion begins with a constitutional requirement for a federal balanced budget."

The GOP promoted cuts, or delegation to states, in programs that directly reduce economic inequality by providing benefits to poor and working Americans. The GOP promoted increases to defense budgets and construction projects, which increasingly consist of contracts for goods and services given to large corporations. And the Party pro-moted a balanced budget that would have inevitably squeezed all dis-cretionary spending other than defense.

Remarkably, despite years of full control of Congress, none of these ideals was realized and none of these proposals was implemented. However, executive orders issued in August, 2020 included a payroll tax holiday - essentially an interest-free loan that would have to be paid back less than two months after the election. With this order, funding of Social Security and Medicare was temporarily suspended.

Full implementation of these proposals would *reduce* the freedom of seniors to choose Medicare coverage, *increase* the freedom of cor-porations and wealthy people to retain more of their income, and *limit* the ability of the federal government to safeguard the freedom of citizens against discriminatory state policies.

The GOP thinks that taking away Tiny Tim's crutches will give him the gift of self-reliance and give him the freedom to walk on his own.

~

The Democratic Party platform calls for changes in taxation with an implied net increase, reducing spending only on the military budget, and increasing spending on other programs across the breadth of the budget - and their platform reflects the recognition of extreme and growing economic inequality.

Democrats call for both tax cuts and tax increases. Here are the planks that promote *reductions* in taxes.

> "We will expand effective tax credits that support domestic manufacturing and grow rural manufacturing jobs through investments in bio-based manufacturing."

> "We will create a new tax credit of up to $15,000 to help first-time homebuyers, and will make the tax credit refundable and advanceable, so buyers can get assistance at the time of purchase....."

> "We will expand the Low-Income Housing Tax Credit to incentivize private-sector construction of affordable housing, and make sure urban, suburban, and rural areas all benefit."

"Democrats will make major investments in quality, affordable child care, including by significantly increasing the Child and Dependent Care Tax Credit....."

"Democrats will... reduce barriers for working families to benefit from targeted tax breaks, including the Earned Income Tax Credit and the Child Tax Credit."

"Our program of reform will provide immediate, marked relief for working families, including more generous, refundable tax credits to benefit low- and middle income families, and easier and more equitable access to tax provisions that help working families build wealth, including by equalizing tax benefits for retirement contributions and providing more accessible tax breaks for homeownership."

"Democrats will provide substantially higher levels of support for programs and institutions that boost economic development in America's most impoverished communities, including by doubling funding for CDFIs, expanding the Community Development Block Grant, increasing the number of Rural Business Investment Companies, and expanding and making permanent the New Markets Tax Credit."

"We will also help Americans pay for long-term care by creating a tax credit for informal and family caregivers and increasing the Child and Dependent Care Tax Credit."

"We will expand access to tax-advantaged ABLE savings accounts, which provide people with disabilities a way to pay for disability-related expenses like housing, education, and transportation."

"Democrats will also take steps to ease the burden of high monthly student loan payments by pausing monthly billing and stopping interest from accruing on federal student loans for people earning less than $25,000, and capping payments at no more than five percent of discretionary income for those earning more than $25,000. After 20 years, remaining federal student loan debt should be automatically forgiven without tax liability."

Of course there are the planks that promote *increases* in taxes.

"Democrats will take action to reverse the Trump Administration's tax cuts benefiting the wealthiest Americans....."

"We will make sure investors pay the same tax rates as workers and bring an end to expensive and unproductive tax loopholes, including the carried interest loophole."

"Corporate tax rates, which were cut sharply by the 2017 Republican tax cut, must be raised....."

"Estate taxes should also be raised back to the historical norm."

"And we will eliminate tax breaks for prescription drug advertisements."

All of the tax changes would have the net effect of reducing levels of economic inequality. But what about spending? Here are the areas that are targeted for increases.

"Democrats believe we must reverse decades of underinvestment in America's public health infrastructure. We will substantially increase funding for the Centers for Disease Control and Prevention (CDC) and for state and local public health departments, many of which suffered deep budget cuts during the Great Recession and are at risk of further cuts....."

"Democrats will support medical and public health research grants for Historically Black Colleges and Universities (HBCUs) and other Minority-Serving Institutions (MSIs), which are particularly well suited to research health disparities in the context of COVID-19."

"Democrats believe we must act immediately to make ambitious investments that will support and create jobs. We urgently need to support state and local governments, which are suffering severe budget shortfalls due to declines in tax revenues while being asked to shoulder the burden of COVID-related services and rising unemployment."

"Democrats stand ready to take immediate, decisive action to pull the economy out of President Trump's recession by investing in infrastructure, care work, clean energy, and small businesses to put Americans to work in good-paying jobs....."

"Democrats will support the most historically far reaching public investments and private sector incentives for research, development, demonstration, and deployment of next-generation technologies, once again making the United States the world's leader in innovation."

"Democrats will increase investments to help state and local governments upgrade election technology, including cybersecurity technology....."

"Democrats will support investments to help the U.S. territories recover from recent natural disasters and build increased resilience to the impacts of climate change, including by expanding access to clean, affordable, reliable energy and water systems."

"We will need increased investments in public education to help students get back on track when public health experts determine it is safe to return to schools."

"We will increase investments in high-quality science, technology, engineering, and mathematics programs in our public schools....."

"Democrats will support and invest in long overdue reforms to make the State Department more strategic, modern, agile, and effective."

"...we will invest in [veterans'] mental health and suicide prevention services, and work with our military communities to encourage and support those seeking help, connecting them to critical services....."

With the exception of domestic manufacturing subsidies and State Department reforms, each of these spending increases is likely to reduce economic inequality. But do Democrats ever promote spending cuts?

"We can maintain a strong defense and protect our safety and security for less. It's past time to rebalance our investments, improve the efficiency and competitiveness of our defense

industrial base, conduct rigorous annual audits of the
Pentagon, and end waste and fraud."

Full implementation of these proposals would *increase* the freedom of
those in disadvantaged communities, *decrease* the freedom of corporations and wealthy people to retain more of their income, and
expand the ability of the federal government to safeguard the freedom
of citizens against discriminatory state policies.

The Democratic platform offers numerous patches and fixes to a
system that fundamentally favors capital over labor and corporations
over people. But patches and fixes may be insufficient when they
completely ignore the fundamental causes of economic inequality -
such fundamental causes as *subsidizing capital* and *taxing the employment of
labor.*

Corporations, Citizenship, Equality, and Freedom

The GOP platform reflected the belief that America's human citizens
don't need federal assistance, but that its corporate citizens do. And
then corporate citizens must be left alone, unregulated, to exercise
their freedom. This, despite the fact that the world's ten largest
corporations are American!

> "Private investment is a key driver of economic growth and
> job creation."

> "Competitiveness equals jobs. That equation governs our
> policies regarding U.S. corporations in the global economy."

> "We propose to level the international playing field by
> lowering the corporate tax rate to be on a par with, or below,
> the rates of other industrial nations."

> "We need to consider the effect of capital gains rates on the
> availability of venture capital, as well as the positive impact of
> expensing on start-up firms."

> "This means relieving the burden and expense of punishing
> government regulations."

> "We support repeal of federal restrictions on political parties
> in McCain-Feingold, raising or repealing contribution limits,

protecting the political speech of advocacy groups,
corporations, and labor unions, and protecting political speech
on the internet."

American corporations, is seems, need federal assistance in taking care
of their own interests. They already enjoy a special status in law, taxation, capital formation, and commerce due to their scale relative to
natural persons, and to their potentially indefinite life span.

The personhood of corporations is implicit in the platform's promotion of their right to freedom of political speech. The juxtaposition
of advocacy groups and labor unions obscures the enormous gap in
available resources between corporations and these other collectives;
after all, money is speech - as ruled by a conservative court. This may
lead to the false equivalency of assuming that all collectives enjoy *the
same* freedom of speech.

The 2016 GOP platform continues to clamor for corporate tax cuts
and continued regulatory relief, despite the incumbent administration's
record of cuts and rollbacks that many believe have irrevocably
damaged the economy and exacerbated economic inequality.

~

The Democratic Party platform reflects the belief that corporations
ought to be regulated and subordinated to the interests of natural
persons. It doesn't shy away from manipulation of corporate behavior
through incentives, penalties, and regulation.

> "Money is not speech, and corporations are not people."

> "We will impose rigorous oversight on big corporations
> seeking financial assistance to weather the pandemic and
> President Trump's recession, to ensure that federal dollars
> support keeping workers on payroll, not enriching CEOs or
> shareholders."

> "Taxpayer money should not be used to pay out dividends,
> fund stock buybacks, or give raises to executives."

> "Democrats commit to forging a new social and economic
> contract with the American people - a contract that invests in
> the people and promotes shared prosperity, not one that
> benefits only big corporations and the wealthiest few."

"If companies shut down their operations here and outsource jobs, we'll claw back any public investments or benefits they received from taxpayers."

"We will crack down on overseas tax havens and close loopholes that are exploited by the wealthiest Americans and biggest corporations."

"...as a last resort, regulators should consider breaking up corporations if they find they are using their market power to engage in anti-competitive activities."

"Democrats will fight to pass a Constitutional amendment that will go beyond merely overturning Citizens United and related decisions like Buckley v. Valeo by eliminating all private financing from federal elections."

Remarkably, both parties agree that the federal government has an active role to play with respect to American corporations. The GOP throws the weight of public policy squarely behind corporate interests; Democrats would use federal resources to control big businesses and subsidize small businesses.

Workers, Labor, Equality, and Freedom

Do working Americans enjoy equality and freedom? What public policies should be in place to ensure the proper place of labor in the national economy? Here's what the Republican Party had to say.

"Minimum wage is an issue that should be handled at the state and local level."

"We support the right of states to enact Right-to-Work laws and call for a national law to protect the economic liberty of the modern workforce."

"The unionization of the federal workforce, first permitted by Democrat presidents in the 1960s, should be reviewed by the appropriate congressional committees to examine its effects on the cost, quality, and performance of the civil service."

> "We renew our call for repeal of the Davis-Bacon law, which
> limits employment and drives up construction and
> maintenance costs for the benefit of unions."

Where opportunities have presented themselves, the incumbent administration has taken action - particularly against the collective bargaining rights of federal employees. The organizing and administrative activities of unions representing federal employees were curtailed by executive orders signed in May, 2018. Implementation was delayed until October, 2019 when a US Court of Appeals injunction expired, and then pursued vigorously by the Office of Personnel Management. Other executive action was taken to promote the use of performance metrics at the VA and to simplify the termination of managers found to be below standards. [6]

Remarkably, the GOP positioned itself as an advocate of workers - an advocacy that consistently emphasized *freedom* over *equality* of bargaining power. Proposing the repeal of the federal minimum wage, for example, was proffered as the way to give workers the freedom to negotiate any wage they choose without a floor on the range.

Placing additional constraints on organized labor likewise focused on workers' freedom from paying union dues. The call for a national Right-to-Work Law referred explicitly to *economic liberty* while ignoring the effect of such laws on wage levels and the relative inequality of bargaining power between labor and management. The GOP's strategy necessarily requires the exposure of the underlying assumption that *organized labor is the enemy of workers*. This is part of a consistent but deceptive narrative that attempts to align the Party with wage earners.

While union members may believe that organized labor serves their interests and the interests of the US economy by helping equalize negotiating power and by reducing inequality, *the GOP disagrees*. Assaulting unions is good for the Party, and it's essential to convince the workers in its rank and file that their interests are somehow served by the assaults.

~

The Democratic platform calls for a raising the minimum wage, the reversal of the gains made by management at the expense of labor, renewed support of labor unions, and the investment of public funds to create job opportunities.

> "Democrats will fight to raise wages for working people and improve job quality and security, including by raising the federal minimum wage to $15 an hour."

> "We will increase funding and staffing at the Department of Labor to aggressively enforce wage, hour, health, and safety rules across the economy."

> "We will enforce labor and environmental protections for farmworkers, including overtime and safety rules....."

> "We will prevent employers from taking advantage of immigrant workers by supporting the Domestic Workers' Bill of Rights and the Protect Our Workers from Exploitation and Retaliation (POWER) Act."

> "We will reform the current unemployment insurance system to enable more workers to remain attached to their jobs, including by promoting payroll support and work-sharing programs with generous rates of wage replacement and requirements that employers maintain workers' benefits."

Clearly improvements in the wages, benefits, and working conditions of American workers enjoy a prominent place in the Democratic Party platform. Democrats view any economic gains made by American workers as equitable, and likely to reduce inequality. More explicitly, labor organizations are seen as essential to realize these gains. But the organizing process itself transfers a measure of freedom from the individual to his union on the day he joins. Do the gains in equality justify the sacrifice of freedom?

> "We know that strong American labor unions help increase wages and job standards for workers across the economy, which is why Democrats will prioritize passing the PRO Act and restoring workers' rights, including the right to launch secondary boycotts."

> "Democrats will recognize unions with majority sign-up - via "card check" processes - and ban captive audience meetings....."

> "Public school educators should have the same rights to organize, join a union, and collectively bargain as private sector workers. Democrats will fight to significantly increase pay and benefits for all educators....."
>
> "Democrats will strengthen labor rights for the more than 20 million public-sector employees in the United States by passing the Public Sector Freedom to Negotiate Act....."
>
> "All jobs in the clean energy economy should provide an opportunity to join a union."

Perhaps most remarkably, the platform calls for the revival of a job corps reminiscent of the Civilian Conservation Corps of the New Deal.

> "Democrats will also mobilize a diverse new generation of young workers through a corps and cohort challenged to conserve our public lands; deliver new clean energy, including to low-income communities and communities of color; and address the changing climate, including through pre-apprenticeship opportunities, joint labor-management registered apprenticeships for training, and direct-hire programs that put good-paying and union jobs within reach for more Americans."

With regard to the interests of labor and working people, the platforms of both parties support the reputation that each of them has earned. For a century, the GOP has been the party of big-money corporate interests and the Democrats have groomed their image as the party of working people. The GOP platform calls for helping corporations; the Democratic platform calls for helping workers. The implications for economic inequality are unmistakable.

Other Inequalities

The GOP platform fosters inequality in many other ways. It called for resource exploitation on Indian reservations, to the benefit of corporations at the expense of some of the neediest among us. It called for privatizing public lands and assets, to the benefit of state and local interests at the expense of the common good. It called for publicly-financed alternatives to public schools, to the benefit of students from wealthy families at the expense of public education. It set the table to replace income taxes with consumption taxes, benefiting investors at the expense of consumers. It supported voter ID laws that are now used to keep poor and minority voters from the polls, to the benefit of incumbent regimes at the expense of democracy.

~

The Democratic platform calls for greater equality in many other ways. Voting rights, the reversal of Citizens United, racial and gender equality of opportunity, and criminal justice reform all have an impact on economic inequality. And while much of this policy positioning is just window dressing, it at least reflects an awareness that the interests of America's real, human citizens must be represented by the policies of one of the major political parties.

Read the platforms for yourself and understand how their positions define *what and who* each of the parties stands for. Economic equality is an aggregation of issues that illustrates the enormous differences between Republicans and Democrats.

EQUALITY AND FREEDOM

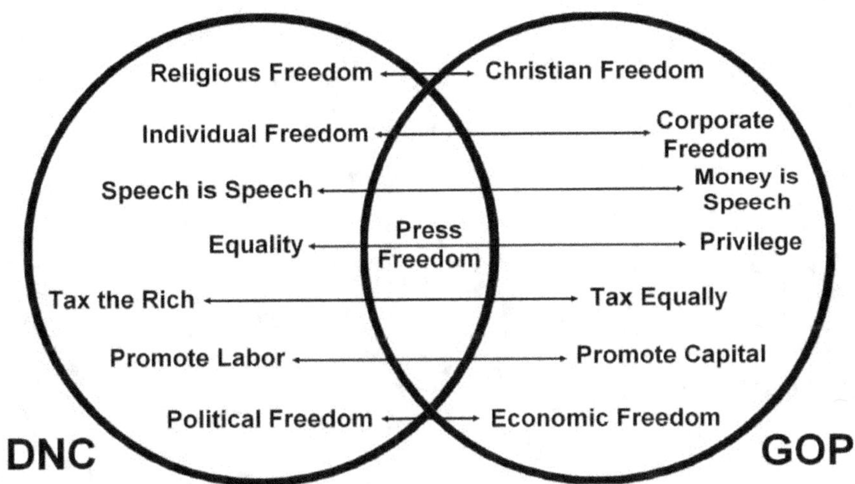

Each party promotes the interests and protects the rights of a different constituency. To the degree that a platform proves an honest and genuine guide to public policy proposals, we can determine for ourselves if our values and interests are fairly represented by our own party.

[1] https://medium.com/@brennanstark/equality-vs-freedom-why-they-cant-coexist-68a36d5dd9aa

[2] http://incitejournal.com/opinion/the-freedom-vs-equality-debate-is-a-false-dichotomy/

[3] http://www.differencebetween.net/language/difference-between-right-and-freedom/

[4] https://www.truthorfiction.com/gideons-military-bases/

[5] https://www.nytimes.com/2020/07/16/us/politics/pompeo-human-rights-policy.html

[6] https://federalnewsnetwork.com/workforce/2019/10/with-injunction-lifted-opm-tells-agencies-to-implement-trumps-workforce-executive-orders/

Human Rights and Civil Rights

Human Rights

Make no mistake - there is a difference between the policy platforms of the Republican Party and the Democratic Party. In recent years, human rights have come under much greater scrutiny as a conesequence of the administration's positions and initiatives on immigration, sanctuary, citizenship, torture, and law enforcement. Here we will draw a distinction between human rights and civil rights.

> "Human rights are rights inherent to all human beings, whatever our nationality, place of residence, sex, national or ethnic origin, colour, religion, language, or any other status. We are all equally entitled to our human rights without discrimination. These rights are all interrelated, interdependent and indivisible." [1]

In 1948 The United Nations adopted The Universal Declaration of Human Rights. This declaration enumerated five specific rights and freedoms, as follows.

> Article 1 - Right to Equality
>
> Article 2 - Freedom from Discrimination
>
> Article 3 -Right to Life, Liberty, Personal Security
>
> Article 4 - Freedom from Slavery
>
> Article 5 - Freedom from Torture and Degrading Treatment

Human rights are regarded as universal, and accorded by god, a creator, or nature. They are not dependent upon nationality, citizenship, or place of residence.

The Republican Party platform eschewed the UN definition of human rights and looked elsewhere - to the US Constitution, as interpreted through the lens of originalism.

> "We affirm - as did the Declaration of Independence: that all are created equal, endowed by their Creator with inalienable

rights of life, liberty, and the pursuit of happiness." "We believe the Constitution was written not as a flexible document, but as our enduring covenant." "We affirm that all legislation, regulation, and official actions must conform to the Constitution's original meaning as understood at the time the language was adopted."

An originalist interpretation of the US Constitution, as that interpretation has evolved today, presents some inescapable discords. The right to equality is tempered by the need to perpetuate generational wealth in order to maintain shareholder value and the quality of western civilization. Freedom from discrimination is subject to the economic freedom of those who might find it profitable to discriminate. Personal security might be vulnerable to suspension for those with insufficient claim to legitimate residency. Freedom from slavery might be suspended for those convicted of a felony. And freedom from torture and degrading treatment might inconvenience intelligence operations at home and abroad.

~

The Democratic Party platform embraces a more modern interpretation of human rights, unbound by the personal perspective of the Founders. The Democrats' interpretation of human rights is much more consonant with that of the global community. We've seen that *equality* is a closely held value. Believing in the universal equality of all people allows the Party to embrace freedom from discrimination, the right to life, liberty, and personal security, freedom from slavery, and freedom from torture and degrading treatment.

> "We will never amplify or legitimize the voices of bigotry, racism, misogyny, anti-Semitism, Islamophobia, or white supremacy. Democrats will protect and promote the equal rights of all our citizens - women, LGBTQ+ people, religious minorities, people with disabilities, Native Americans, and all who have been discriminated against in too many ways and for too many generations."

> "We will stand up to the forces of authoritarianism, not aid and abet their rise, and we will speak and act with clarity and purpose on behalf of human rights wherever they are under threat."

"Democrats believe that freedom of religion is a fundamental human right, and we will never use protection of that right as a cover for discrimination."

"Democrats believe that torture is immoral and ineffective."

"Every American has the right to breathe clean air, drink clean water, and live without fear of exposure to toxic waste."

"Democrats believe health care is a human right."

"Democrats will always protect sexual and reproductive health and rights."

"We will negotiate strong and enforceable standards for labor, human rights, and the environment in the core text of our trade deals."

"And we will act expeditiously to reinstate Department of Education guidance protecting transgender students' rights under Title IX and make clear that schools shall not discriminate based on LGBTQ+ status."

"We will rejoin and reform the WHO, the United Nations Human Rights Council, and the United Nations Population Fund....."

"We will restore the United States' position of leadership on LGBTQ+ issues by passing the GLOBE Act and appointing senior leaders directly responsible for driving and coordinating LGBTQ+ issues at the State Department, USAID, and the National Security Council. We will ensure that our immigration policies account for the needs of LGBTQ+ refugees and asylum seekers, and that we use the full slate of human rights promotion and accountability tools to defend the universal rights of LGBTQ+ people. We will amplify the voices of LGBTQ+ persons around the world and counter violence and discrimination against LGBTQ+ persons wherever it appears."

Civil Rights

Civil rights may be viewed as separate and distinct from human rights. In reality, they are an extension of human rights that are conferred upon citizens by a government. Of course, all citizens are also persons, but not all persons are citizens. Similarly, all human rights are also civil rights, but not all civil rights are human rights.

Civil rights, for our purposes, include civil liberties without distinction. In addition to the human rights guaranteed to all persons, citizens may enjoy the right to vote, the right to a fair trial, the right to a public education, and the right of access to public goods and facilities. Civil rights might be extended or denied to groups and identities such as labor, corporations, women, and minorities. Civil rights legislation has established our right to marry whom we choose, equal treatment under the law, privacy, and has reinforced our freedom from discrimination - a *human* right.

Voting Rights

Dr. Martin Luther King argued that without voting rights, all other rights are meaningless. Predictably, the two party platforms stand in stark contrast. Republicans championed the right of big-money interests to influence elections, opposed the direct popular vote, and promoted local restrictions on polling through voter ID, proof of citizenship, and other measures.

> "Freedom of speech includes the right to devote resources to whatever cause or candidate one supports. We oppose any restrictions or conditions that would discourage citizens from participating in the public square or limit their ability to promote their ideas, such as requiring private organizations to publicly disclose their donors to the government."

> "We support repeal of federal restrictions on political parties in McCain-Feingold, raising or repealing contribution limits, protecting the political speech of advocacy groups, corporations, and labor unions, and protecting political speech on the internet."

> "We pledge to restore the proper balance and vertical separation of powers between the federal government and state governments....."

> "We oppose the National Popular Vote Interstate Compact and any other scheme to abolish or distort the procedures of the Electoral College."

> "…we support legislation to require proof of citizenship when registering to vote and secure photo ID when voting."

> "…we urge our elected representatives to ensure that citizenship, rather than mere residency, be made the basis for the apportionment of representatives among the states."

Each of these planks in some way either diminishes the power of individuals' vote or increases the difficulty of certain classes of natural persons to cast their ballots.

The last of these planks deals indirectly with voting rights. The US Constitution requires a census every ten years consisting of a count of *persons* rather than *citizens*. The census is then used as the basis for appointment of representatives among the states. The GOP's departure from this constitutional principle creates a conflict between the Party's platform and their Constitution if the latter is to be interpreted according to *originalist doctrine*. Perhaps counting citizens rather than persons serves the Party's interest.

~

Democrats champion the removal of big-money influence from the electoral process, and promote measures to guarantee access to the voting booth regardless of race, color, age demographic, or income. In response to the US Supreme Court decision in Shelby County v Holder, the subsequent actions taken by conservative states - and the narrative of the incumbent Republican administration - the Democratic platform has *a lot* to say.

> "We will restore the full power of the Voting Rights Act and stamp out voter suppression in all its forms."

> "Democrats are committed to restoring the full power of the Voting Rights Act and ensuring every citizen can access the ballot box."

"We will curb the corrupting influence of money in politics and protect the integrity of our elections from all enemies, foreign and domestic."

"The formerly incarcerated should not be blocked from exercising their voting rights or accessing public services, including Pell Grants and nutrition assistance, available to other free citizens of the United States."

"Democrats will restore the full powers of the Voting Rights Act and go further to roll back discriminatory policies that have been put in place in recent years to prevent people of color from voting."

"We will ensure all federal agencies produce materials in languages commonly spoken in the United States, including languages spoken by Asian American and Pacific Islander communities, and that voting materials are also easily accessible for citizens with limited English proficiency."

"Democrats are committed to the sacred principle of 'one person, one vote' - and we will fight to achieve that principle for every citizen, regardless of race, income, disability status, geography, or English language proficiency."

"We stand united against the determined Republican campaign to disenfranchise voters through onerous voter ID laws, unconstitutional and excessive purges of the voter rolls, and closures of polling places in low-income neighborhoods, on college campuses, and in communities of color."

"Americans should never have to wait in hours-long lines to exercise their voting rights."

"We will make it a priority to... ensure the Department of Justice challenges state laws that make it harder for Americans to vote."

"We will make voting easier and more accessible for all Americans by supporting automatic voter registration, same-day voter registration, early voting, and universal vote-from-home and vote-by-mail options."

"Democrats believe Election Day should be a national holiday, in celebration of our democratic institutions and to make it easier for everyone to cast their ballot."

"We will fully implement the Help America Vote Act and require that polling places and elections are accessible for people with disabilities, and work to ensure that returning citizens have their voting rights restored upon release from jail or prison."

"Democrats unequivocally support statehood for Washington, D.C., so the citizens of the District can at last have full and equal representation in Congress and the rights of self-determination."

The motivation of each party may be found in the demographics each serves. The GOP expressly serves the interests of property and business, and an advantage can be gained by preventing poor people and minorities from voting. Democrats expressly serve poor people, working people, and minorities, so it makes sense for them to maximize the number and impact of these votes. Although there may be high principles at the root of each party's approach, there's also the component of self-interest.

Labor rights

Republicans and Democrats couldn't be more divergent in their approach to labor. The GOP has always identified with management, and in recent years has stepped up its campaign against organized labor. Their 2016 platform has driven the policy of the current administration, in both words and actions. The platform said this.

"Although unionization has never been permitted in any government agency concerned with national security, the current [prior] Administration has reversed that policy for the Transportation Security Administration. We will correct that mistake"

"We support the right of states to enact Right-to-Work laws and call for a national law to protect the economic liberty of the modern workforce"

"A Republican administration should streamline personnel procedures to expedite the firing of bad workers, tax cheats, and scammers."

"The unionization of the federal workforce, first permitted by Democrat presidents in the 1960s, should be reviewed by the appropriate congressional committees to examine its effects on the cost, quality, and performance of the civil service."

Where opportunities have presented themselves, the incumbent administration has taken action. We've seen that the organizing and administrative activities of unions representing federal employees were curtailed by executive orders signed in May, 2018 and implemented in 2019 following legal challenges. Other executive action was taken simplify the termination of managers found to be below standards - an action that was met with uncharacteristically bipartisan approval. [2] The administration has done little more to promote these planks.

~

Historically, Democrats have championed the worker and organized labor, if not consistently. The right to organize or join a union is seen as a civil right to be extended to all citizens.

"Democrats commit to forging a new social and economic contract with the American people - a contract that..... raises wages and restores workers' rights to organize, join a union, and collectively bargain....."

"We know that strong American labor unions help increase wages and job standards for workers across the economy, which is why Democrats will prioritize passing the PRO Act and restoring workers' rights, including the right to launch secondary boycotts."

"Democrats will recognize unions with majority sign-up - via "card check" processes - and ban captive audience meetings....."

"Public school educators should have the same rights to organize, join a union, and collectively bargain as private sector workers."

"We will condition state and federal aid on maintaining and expanding public-sector employment, including provisions to protect workers' rights."

"We believe all employers funded by taxpayer dollars must pay their workers at least $15 an hour and protect workers' rights to organize."

Do *civil rights* include the right of collective bargaining? The two parties offer opposing viewpoints that reflect the contrast in their values, beliefs - and their constituencies.

Business and Property Rights

The GOP perceived emerging threats to "economic freedom" which in turn threaten political freedom. Personal data and intellectual property rights are really corporate issues accruing to the interests of technology and drug companies.

"We believe political freedom and economic freedom are indivisible. When political freedom and economic freedom are separated - both are in peril; when united, they are invincible."

"We call on any state legislatures that have not already done so to nullify the impact of Kelo within their jurisdiction by legislation or state constitutional amendments declaring Republicans in supporting the Private Property Rights Protection Act."

"We call for strong action by Congress and a new Republican president to enforce intellectual property laws against all infringers, whether foreign or domestic."

"We will ensure that personal data receives full constitutional protection from government overreach. The only way to safeguard or improve these systems is through the private sector."

Kelo v. New London was an action brought against the City of New London in 2004 in response to its seizure of private property for, in its view, the common economic good. The US Supreme Court found that the seizure of property for "public use" was justified even though access to the property was not directly available to the public. [3]

Clearly, this plank calls for expanded rights to private property and protections against the exercise of eminent domain.

Intellectual property laws accrue primarily to the benefit of corporations. Such laws deal with copyrights, patents, and administrative procedures and serve to protect monopolies against competition. The terms and conditions of intellectual property laws have been expanded and extended in recent decades. Enterprises ranging from entertainment to pharmaceuticals to computer technology can easily extend their monopolies by decades simply by making minor changes in packaging, platforms, or delivery media.

Personal data has been vigorously protected by the incumbent administration - provided that it's the data of the incumbent administration or its allies. Others, including journalists, users of social media, and bloggers, may have received less protection as federal agencies have ramped up their investigations of the administration's political enemies.

~

The Democratic Party platform fails to address business and property rights at all, perhaps assuming that such rights are already adequately protected.

Minority Rights

Noble language clouds the contrast between the meanings of the parties' policy platforms, especially with respect to minority rights. Careful reading of the GOP platform reveals hidden intent that serves to protect the supremacy of the majority rather than the rights of any minority.

> "We denounce bigotry, racism, anti-Semitism, ethnic prejudice, and religious intolerance."

> "We continue to encourage equality for all citizens and access to the American Dream. Merit and hard work should determine advancement in our society, so we reject unfair preferences, quotas, and set-asides as forms of discrimination."

"…five unelected lawyers robbed 320 million Americans of their legitimate constitutional authority to define marriage as the union of one man and one woman."

"We endorse the First Amendment Defense Act, Republican legislation in the House and Senate which will bar government discrimination against individuals and businesses for acting on the belief that marriage is the union of one man and one woman."

"To protect everyone - and especially the most vulnerable: children, women, and elders - the legal system in tribal communities must provide stability and protect property rights."

"[Title IX] is now being used by bureaucrats to impose a social and cultural revolution upon the American people by wrongly redefining sex discrimination to include sexual orientation or other categories."

"The Republican Party, a party of law and order, must make clear in words and action that every human life matters."

"With the murder rate soaring in our great cities, we condemn the Supreme Court's erosion of the right of the people to enact capital punishment in their states."

There's some fluff here, and we can skip that. But rejecting "unfair preferences, quotas, and set-asides" refers to affirmative action - and it ignores centuries of minority repression that's reflected in today's economic realities. The platform champions the right of a business to discriminate based on sexual orientation or its own definition of marriage. It promotes the exploitation of Native American tribal resources. It promotes a system of capital punishment that disproportionately kills people of color.

Perhaps most remarkably, the GOP platform discounted the emergent Black Lives Matter movement by picking up the "all lives matter" slogan so often shouted by white supremacists. This is all the more remarkable in light of the national awakening in 2020 to police violence against people of color and the larger impact of the criminal justice establishment upon minority citizens. For many Americans, the *party of law and order* has become the party of oppression and protofascism.

The record of the incumbent Republican administration has not been kind to minorities. Continuing claims that black and Latino communities have benefited from GOP economic policies are far better explained by the business cycle than by the causal relationship of policies. Of course, that's just a dim memory in the rubbish heap of the economic effects of the pandemic.

~

Democrats have a different view. Implicit in the Party's view of *equality* is that minorities - *all minorities* - enjoy the same rights and privileges afforded to all citizens. Consequently, the platform is focused on specific issues such as economic opportunity, police brutality, housing, and education.

> "Democrats commit to forging a new social and economic contract with the American people - a contract that... at last grapples honestly with America's long and ongoing history of racism and disenfranchisement, of segregation and discrimination, and invests instead in building equity and mobility for the people of color who have been left out and left behind for generations."

> "Democrats are committed to standing up to racism and bigotry in our laws, in our culture, in our politics, and in our society, and recognize that race-neutral policies are not sufficient to rectify race-based disparities. We will take a comprehensive approach to embed racial justice in every element of our governing agenda, including in jobs and job creation, workforce and economic development, small business and entrepreneurship, eliminating poverty and closing the racial wealth gap, promoting asset building and homeownership, education, health care, criminal justice reform, environmental justice, and voting rights."

> "We believe Black lives matter, and will establish a national commission to examine the lasting economic effects of slavery, Jim Crow segregation, and racially discriminatory federal policies on income, wealth, educational, health, and

employment outcomes; to pursue truth and promote racial healing; and to study reparations."

"Democrats also support measures to increase diversity among the ranks of police departments, so our law enforcement agencies look more like the communities they serve."

"Instead of making evidence-based investments in education, jobs, health care, and housing that are proven to keep communities safe and prevent crime from occurring in the first place, our system has criminalized poverty, overpoliced and underserved Black and brown communities, and cut public services."

"It is unacceptable that Black parents must have "the talk" with their children, to try to protect them from the very police officers who are supposed to be sworn to protect and serve them. It is unacceptable that more than 1,000 people, a quarter of them Black, have been killed by police every year since 2015."

"We will confront white nationalist terrorism and combat hate crimes perpetrated against religious minorities."

"We will equalize access to affordable credit and improve access to down payment assistance to help families of color, low-income families, and rural buyers purchase homes."

"Democrats support appointing judges who will enforce the Civil Rights Act in schools and will fund magnet schools and school transportation initiatives to help facilitate improved integration."

"We will also reinvigorate and increase funding for the Department of Education's Office of Civil Rights and improve federal data collection on racial segregation in schools."

"We will break the school-to-prison pipeline that sees children of color disproportionately punished by the criminal justice system for disciplinary issues that should be handled by school administrators or counselors"

"Democrats will create an environmental justice fund to make historic investments aimed at eliminating legacy pollution, which disproportionately causes illness and premature death in communities of color, low-income communities, and Indigenous communities."

"Democrats will maintain the legal requirement for Census participation and increase resources to reduce undercounts of communities of color, immigrants, LGBT people, people with disabilities, rural and low-income populations, and young children that have long plagued the decennial Census."

"...we must prioritize STEAM education and funding for underrepresented students, including students of color, girls, and low-income students, to help reduce enrollment and achievement gaps."

"Democrats recognize and support the sovereignty of Tribal Nations and pledge to work on a nation-to-nation basis to empower Indigenous peoples, increase economic development in Tribal Nations, and protect Tribal lands, assets, resources, and treaty rights."

The Democratic platform explicitly refers to minorities, and acknowledges the reality of discrimination in 2020. It recognizes the Black Lives Matter movement as rooted in bona fide civil rights issues. It promotes criminal justice reform, and recognizes that racial minorities will be the beneficiaries of that reform.

Religious Rights

The parties rarely agree, but on religion they are united - religious faith and religious institutions are to be favored in American law and culture. But differences exist in their approaches. Republicans explicitly promoted God's word above the Constitution.

"The Declaration [of Independence] sets forth the fundamental precepts of American government: That God bestows certain inalienable rights on every individual, thus producing human equality; that government exists first and foremost to protect those inalienable rights; that man-made law must be consistent with God-given, natural rights; and that if God-given, natural, inalienable rights come in conflict

with government, court, or human-granted rights, God-given,
natural, inalienable rights always prevail; that there is a moral
law recognized as 'the Laws of Nature and of Nature's
God…..'"

"We support laws to confirm the longstanding American
tradition that religious individuals and institutions can educate
young people, receive government benefits, and participate in
public debates without having to check their religious beliefs at
the door."

"The government cannot use subsequent amendments to limit
First Amendment rights."

"We support the right of the people to conduct their
businesses in accordance with their religious beliefs"

"We pledge to defend the religious beliefs and rights of
conscience of all Americans and to safeguard religious
institutions against government control."

"We support the public display of the Ten
Commandments…"

Remarkably, religious rights were extended to corporations as well as
people, which explicitly placed them above secular law. The platform
also clarified which family of religions it's promoting in its support for
the public display of the Ten Commandments.

The pledge to protect religion from government begs the question,
who will safeguard government against religious control?

~

The Democratic Party platform is decidedly more secular; the entire
platform contains but a single reference to God. Democrats explicitly
regard religious freedom as a *human* right rather than just a *civil* right.
And using religious rights as an excuse for corporations and other
organizations to discriminate against others is explicitly repudiated.

"Democrats believe that freedom of religion is a fundamental
human right, and we will never use protection of that right as a
cover for discrimination."

"Democrats will protect and promote the equal rights of…
religious minorities….."

"We will confront white nationalist terrorism and combat hate crimes perpetrated against religious minorities."

"Democrats will also work to restore trust with our Muslim communities by ensuring the government's engagement is not discriminatory nor viewed through a security lens."

"We will reverse discriminatory [immigration] bans and policies that deny protection to groups based on their religion or sexual orientation."

"We will require officer training in effective nonviolent tactics, appropriate use of force, implicit bias, and peer intervention, both at the academy and on the job. And we will ban racial and religious profiling in law enforcement."

"We will reject the Trump Administration's use of broad religious exemptions to allow businesses, medical providers, social service agencies, and others to discriminate."

Women's' Rights

The platforms couldn't be in greater contrast. The GOP did not acknowledge women's rights anywhere in its 2016 text except for imposing these new limitations.

"We support a human life amendment to the Constitution and legislation to make clear that the Fourteenth Amendment's protections apply to children before birth."

"We will not fund or subsidize health care that includes abortion coverage."

One consequence of these planks and of the values they represented was the appointment of federal justices based in part on their ideological opposition to a woman's right to choose to abort her fetus. The incumbent Republican administration enacted numerous rule changes on federal funding, group health insurance, and the Affordable Care Act that were upheld by a judiciary that is increasingly intolerant of choice.

~

Democrats explicitly enumerate support for existing women's rights and an expansion of those rights in key areas such as economic opportunity, health choices, and freedom from violence. As with all civil rights, equality is respected.

"Democrats will fight to guarantee equal rights for women, including by ratifying the Equal Rights Amendment and at long last enshrining gender equality in the U.S. Constitution."

"Democrats will forge a new social and economic contract with the American people - a contract that... ensures equal pay for women and paid family leave for all....."

"Democrats will take decisive action to level the playing field for people of color, working families, women, and others who have been left on the sidelines."

"We will raise the minimum wage to $15 an hour and guarantee equal pay for women, two measures that in combination will pull millions of families out of poverty."

"Federal contractors should be required to develop and disclose plans to recruit and promote women... - and be held accountable for delivering."

"And we will increase funding for programs supporting businesses owned by women....."

"We will restore federal funding for Planned Parenthood, which provides vital preventive and reproductive health care for millions of women....."

"Democrats oppose and will fight to overturn federal and state laws that create barriers to women's reproductive health and rights. We will repeal the Hyde Amendment, and protect and codify *Roe v. Wade*."

"Democrats will expand postpartum Medicaid coverage to a full year after giving birth, invest in rural maternal health, promote a diverse perinatal workforce, and implement implicit bias training for health professionals."

"Democrats will at last reauthorize the Violence Against Women Act, reaffirm provisions relating to Tribal jurisdiction, and expand the list of crimes that can be prosecuted under the statute to include stalking, child abuse, and trafficking."

The GOP seemed to believe that women as a group do not deserve any special consideration or legal protection. Democrats acknowledge that women are not a minority, but their interests have been historically ignored or violated in American society. Centuries of financial discrimination, disenfranchisement, and violence have had an impact on today's realities and the public policy response of the Democratic platform.

Other Rights

Obvious differences are apparent in the realm of gun rights, education, health care, and sexual orientation. Common interests might be found with regard to citizens with disabilities and special privilege for military veterans. The GOP platform also reflected a concern with privacy of information, offshore financial secrecy, and human trafficking.

> "We uphold the right of individuals to keep and bear arms, a natural inalienable right that predates the Constitution and is secured by the Second Amendment."

> "We condemn frivolous lawsuits against gun manufacturers and the current [prior] Administration's illegal harassment of firearm dealers."

> "We oppose any attempts by government to require surveillance devices in our daily lives, including tracking devices in motor vehicles."

> "Americans overseas should enjoy the same rights as Americans residing in the United States, whose private financial information is not subject to disclosure to the government except as to interest earned."

> "We oppose the non-consensual withholding or withdrawal of care or treatment, including food and water, from individuals with disabilities, newborns, the elderly, or the infirm, just as we oppose euthanasia and assisted suicide."

> "The federal government should not be a partner in [American education], as the Constitution gives it no role in education."

"Any honest agenda for improving health care must start with repeal of the dishonestly named Affordable Care Act of 2010: Obamacare."

"We support the ability of all organizations to provide, purchase, or enroll in health care coverage consistent with their religious, moral, or ethical convictions without discrimination or penalty."

"America's continuing participation in the international campaign against human trafficking merits our support."

"The Individuals with Disabilities Education Act (IDEA) has opened up unprecedented opportunities for many students. Congressional Republicans will lead in its reauthorization, as well as renewal of the Higher Education Act, which can offer students with disabilities increased access to the general curriculum."

"We will retain the preference given to veterans when they seek federal employment."

Gun rights activists have been well represented in the incumbent Republican administration despite the continuing incidence of gun violence and mass shootings. The administration has successfully prevented the restoration of product liability to firearms manufacturers, and has ignored armed protests threatening violence by white nationalists.

Although the GOP platform explicitly opposed the freedom of assisted suicide the federal government has refrained from interfering with the right of states to establish their own policies.

The goal of eliminating the role of the federal government in America's education was addressed with cabinet appointments and appropriations rather than legislation. The Department of Education continues with reduced funding levels, part of which is now allocated to private parochial Christian-religious schools. The department is administered by a campaign contributor and avowed enemy of secular public education.

The GOP platform called for the confirmation of rights granted to organizations - *read corporations* - to adopt and embrace closely held religious beliefs to gain the freedom to discriminate against classes of

employees enrolled in health insurance plans. The incumbent
Republican administration sought to secure and expand proscriptions
against birth control, abortion coverage, and other medical needs.

~

The Democratic platform reflects a belief that health care, housing,
and education are common goods and therefore rank as rights rather
than privileges. Disabled Americans and Native Americans garner
special attention in defense of their rights. Democrats have a lot to say
about gun violence.

> "Gun violence is a public health crisis in the United States."

> "Addressing the gun violence crisis requires supporting
> evidence-based programs that prevent gun deaths from
> occurring in the first place, including by making mental health
> care more accessible, funding interventions to reduce
> homicides and gun violence in neighborhoods, and
> strengthening protections against domestic violence."

> "Democrats will also ensure the Centers for Disease Control
> and Prevention have sufficient resources to study gun violence
> as a public health issue."

> "Democrats will enact universal background checks, end
> online sales of guns and ammunition, close dangerous
> loopholes that currently allow stalkers and some individuals
> convicted of assault or battery to buy and possess firearms,
> and adequately fund the federal background check system. We
> will close the "Charleston loophole" and prevent individuals
> who have been convicted of hate crimes from possessing
> firearms. Democrats will ban the manufacture and sale of
> assault weapons and high capacity magazines. We will
> incentivize states to enact licensing requirements for owning
> firearms and "red flag" laws that allow courts to temporarily
> remove guns from the possession of those who are a danger
> to themselves or others. We will pass legislation requiring that
> guns be safely stored in homes. And Democrats believe that
> gun companies should be held responsible for their products,
> just like any other business, and will prioritize repealing the
> law that shields gun manufacturers from civil liability."

"We must provide a world-class education in every ZIP code, to every child, because education is a critical public good."

"Democrats commit to forging a new social and economic contract with the American people - a contract that... affirms housing is a right and not a privilege....."

"We must guarantee health care not as a privilege for some, but as a right for every single American."

"We will launch our country's second great railroad revolution by investing in high-speed rail, and commit to public transportation as a public good, including ensuring transit jobs are good jobs."

"Democrats will fully enforce the Americans with Disabilities Act, the Individuals with Disabilities Education Act, the Fair Housing Act, the Civil Rights of Institutionalized Persons Act, Section 504 of the Rehabilitation Act, the Mental Health Parity and Addiction Equity Act, and the Help America Vote Act, among other bedrock statutes protecting the rights of people with disabilities."

"Historic wrongs and abuses perpetrated against Native Americans... have created profound and lasting inequities in income, wealth, education, employment, housing, environmental quality, and health care....."

Democrats clearly promote the right of the public to be safe from gun violence even if the rights of gun ownership are regulated; Republicans promote the right of private gun ownership even if the public is endangered.

Read the platforms for yourself and understand how their positions define what and who each of the parties stands for. The issues relating to human rights and civil rights illustrate the enormous differences between Republicans and Democrats. Each party promotes the interests and protects the rights of a different constituency. To the degree that a platform proves an honest and genuine guide to public policy proposals, we can determine for ourselves if our values and interests are fairly represented by our own party.

HUMAN & CIVIL RIGHTS

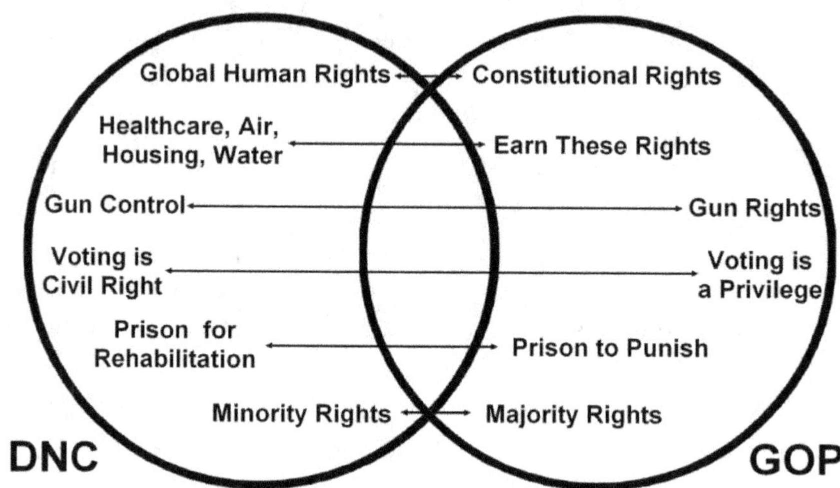

Republicans and Democrats approach human rights and civil rights from divergent positions. Here lie some of the most basic differences between the parties.

[1]
https://www.ohchr.org/en/issues/pages/whatarehumanrights.aspx

[2] https://federalnewsnetwork.com/workforce/2019/10/with-injunction-lifted-opm-tells-agencies-to-implement-trumps-workforce-executive-orders/

[3] https://supreme.justia.com/cases/federal/us/545/469/#tab-opinion-1961893

Science, Energy, and the Environment

Make no mistake - there is a difference between the policy platforms of Republicans and Democrats. The issues surrounding science, public health, technology, energy, and the environment seem to polarize the positions between the parties. Many of these issues have come to light as a consequence of the words and actions of the incumbent Republican administration rather than a platform of policies. These words and actions clearly demonstrate a disregard for science and a reduction of the scientific community's role in public policy.

The following sections feature direct quotations from each of the platforms, together with a little interpretive commentary.

Covid-19 Pandemic

The novel coronavirus pandemic is real, and its ongoing effects now profoundly impact our daily lives. Some of us have lost friends and family to the disease and those among us who have recovered may suffer long-lasting impairments. The economic impact has been greater than anything foreseen in 2016, and much of the damage will be very long lasting.

A platform written four years ago must necessarily remain mute on this most critical public policy issue. Whatever policies and tactics are implemented in the future will continue without the guidance of Republican Party values and strategies.

~

The Democratic Party platform recognizes the reality and impact of the Covid-19 pandemic. It also recognizes the connections the pandemic has clarified between inequality and health outcomes, and proposes specific policies to address the failures and shortcomings of the national health infrastructure.

> "COVID-19 has laid bare deep fault lines in our economy, our society, and our health care system. Disparities in health care

access, in environmental quality, in the employment market, and in housing have contributed to disproportionate rates of infection and death among Black Americans, Native Americans, and Latinos."

"Democrats support making COVID-19 testing, treatment, and any eventual vaccines free to everyone, regardless of their wealth, insurance coverage, or immigration status."

"Democrats believe we must follow the informed advice of scientists and public health experts, and will take steps to protect federal scientists from political influence."

"We must also expand funding so state and local public health departments can hire sufficient staff to conduct contact tracing for everyone who tests positive for the novel coronavirus."

"We will improve oversight and expand protections for residents and staff at nursing homes, which have seen some of the worst COVID-19 outbreaks."

"And we will expand support for telemedicine, so Americans do not have to go without essential health care during the pandemic."

"Democrats will act swiftly to stand up a comprehensive, national public health surveillance program for COVID-19 and future infectious diseases. We will recruit at least 100,000 contact tracers with support from trusted local organizations in the communities most at risk to help state and local health departments use culturally competent approaches to identify people at risk of contracting or spreading the coronavirus."

"We urgently need to support state and local governments, which are suffering severe budget shortfalls due to declines in tax revenues while being asked to shoulder the burden of COVID11 related services and rising unemployment."

"Democrats support making significant, immediate grants and loans to help small businesses make payroll, pay rent and other expenses, and keep their doors open when possible."

We will immediately enact robust paid sick leave protections as part of the COVID-19 response for all workers in the economy, including contractors, gig workers, domestic workers, and the self-employed."

"As the COVID-19 pandemic demonstrates, our country needs the best experts working within government to protect and improve the lives of all Americans. Democrats support the recruitment of people with expertise in science, social science, technology, and innovation to jobs in public service to help solve our nation's most pressing challenges."

"To ensure that federal funds are invested as effectively and efficiently as possible, the federal government should be using the best available evidence when making budget and spending decisions."

Climate Change

Each party deals with this issue from a very different viewpoint. The 2016 GOP platform referred to climate change just seven times, and not one mention acknowledged it as a valid concern, much less as a worthy object of the federal government's attention. In fact, a number of policy positions were stated to oppose existing or proposed measures to address it.

"We oppose any carbon tax."

"We will likewise forbid the EPA to regulate carbon dioxide, something never envisioned when Congress passed the Clean Air Act."

"The United Nations' Intergovernmental Panel on Climate Change is a political mechanism, not an unbiased scientific institution. Its unreliability is reflected in its intolerance toward scientists and others who dissent from its orthodoxy."

"We reject the agendas of both the Kyoto Protocol and the Paris Agreement, which represent only the personal commitments of their signatories….."

"We demand an immediate halt to U.S. funding for the U.N.'s Framework Convention on Climate Change (UNFCCC)….."

The incumbent Republican administration moved quickly and thoroughly to reverse the environmental policies of its predecessors. In November, 2019, the administration served notice of withdrawal from the Paris Agreement on Climate Change, which if implemented would remove the US economy from the largest and most inclusive global environmental and economic collaboration ever seen in peacetime.

The Environmental Protection Agency in 2017 rolled back the Clean Power Plan that would have reduced greenhouse gas emissions from generating plants. The Department of Energy rolled back a 2007 regulation intended to phase out energy-inefficient incandescent light bulbs. The administration refuses to support bipartisan legislation to limit hydrofluorocarbons in accordance with the Kigali Amendment to the Montreal Protocol. In spite of opposition from environmental scientists and industry interests, the EPA rolled back methane pollution rules that applied to oil and gas infrastructure. The EPA in 2020 also loosened vehicle emission standards and the administration even set about to revoke a state's right to establish stricter limits.

~

The Democratic Party continues to regard climate change as an existential threat. Their platform reflects acceptance of the consensus of climate scientists, and proposes specific policy responses. Additionally, the responses in several instances mobilize the labor force to carry out the proposals.

> "We must lead the world in taking on the climate crisis, not deny the science and accelerate the damage."

> "Democrats will rejoin the Paris Climate Agreement and go further, building a thriving, equitable, and globally competitive clean energy economy that puts workers and communities first, and leaves no one behind."

> "Democrats recognize that the United States does not stand alone in the fight against climate change and global environmental degradation."

> "We will repair, modernize, and expand our highways, roads, bridges, and airports, including by installing 500,000 public charging stations for electric vehicles, ensuring our passenger

transportation systems are resilient to the impacts of climate change....."

"Democrats additionally support strengthening NASA and the National Oceanic and Atmospheric Administration's Earth observation missions to better understand how climate change is impacting our home planet."

"We will restore funding to the Global Environment Facility and the Intergovernmental Panel on Climate Change, to support critical climate science research around the world."

The Republican view, largely implemented, was to deny the existence of the issue and to reject or roll back any actions taken by domestic or international public policy. The Democrats' view is to embrace international accords and promote domestic solutions - including the recovery of proven negative economic externalities.

Science and Partnerships

Small-government Republicans were quite willing to delegate federal government prerogatives to private entities. Partnerships often take the form of subsidies, patronage, and payments to such entities and then permitting them to reap the benefits of such patronage without regulation. Science was seen as a good thing if it could be harnessed by private enterprise.

"Technological change drives our positions with regard to STEM education, business and corporate involvement with educational certifications, workforce issues, privacy, cyber and national security, energy development, regulation, and other elements of our campaign for growth and jobs."

"We envision government at all levels as a partner with individuals and industries in technological progress, not a meddlesome monitor."

"We will not tolerate the use of bogus science and scare tactics to bar our products from foreign markets"

"We encourage public-private partnerships to provide predictable support for connecting rural areas so that every American can fully participate in the global economy."

"As incubators of unconventional thinking, our country's existing research infrastructure - the National Labs, the National Institutes of Health, NASA, and elements of the Defense Department - have the potential to form partnerships with small businesses to create an American Start-Up Century."

"The President, the Congress, the Department of Homeland Security, the Department of Defense, the States, the utilities, and the private sector should work together on an urgent basis to enact Republican legislation, pending in both chambers, to protect the national grid [against EMP warfare] and encourage states to take the initiative to protect their own grids expeditiously."

Public-private partnerships - *PPPs* - reflect a core value of the GOP. By outsourcing projects to private corporations - projects that would ordinarily come under the federal domain - government infrastructure can be reduced while simultaneously providing an opportunity for profit to the GOP's constituency.

The most successful PPPs are those that were formed between NASA and private contractors like SpaceX, Ceres Robotics, and Blue Origin. Although many of these partnerships were established during previous administrations, they have been expanded successfully under NASA's *tipping point* program in which 25% or more of a mission is under the control of private enterprise.

Overall, PPPs played a relatively small role in the priorities of the current Republican administration and Congress until 2020. Infra-structure repair and expansion - including data networks and security systems - received a lot of attention but virtually no funding of policy initiatives.

The most prominent partnerships have been failures. In early March, 2020, the administration announced a PPP to expanding testing for Covid-19 rather than empowering federal resources or invoking the Defense Production Act. At least four federal officials were placed in parallel charge of coordinating the partnership, and that certainly con-tributed to its subsequent failure. As the pandemic spread, testing capacity continued woefully insufficient for many months. The financial winners and losers may not be determined for years.

~

Democrats promote public-private partnerships in agricultural science, medicine, cyber-security, research and development, and clean energy. While their platform promotes partnerships with the private sector, it more strongly emphasizes binding relationships with other countries and international institutions, envisioning a more productive partnership with the international scientific community.

> "Democrats will partner with America's farmers, ranchers, and forest landowners to make the U.S. agriculture sector the first in the world to achieve net-zero emissions, which will spark a revolution in agriculture and open up new revenue streams for farmers in energy and waste products, and grow bio-based manufacturing jobs."

> "We will help rebuild our economy... by mobilizing historic, transformative public and private investments to launch a clean energy revolution."

> "Democrats will support the most historically far reaching public investments and private sector incentives for research, development, demonstration, and deployment of next-generation technologies, once again making the United States the world's leader in innovation."

> "Democrats will direct the federal government to work with private-sector manufacturers to dramatically scale up the United States' domestic manufacturing capacity for both personal protective equipment and essential medicines."

> "We will strengthen support for the United States' role in space through our continued presence on the International Space Station, working in partnership with the international community to continue scientific and medical innovation."

> "Democrats will partner with other countries and private companies to build up capacity and implement appropriate safety standards for any work that involves dangerous pathogens, and we remain staunchly committed to the international prohibition on the development or use of biological weapons."

"Democrats will maintain American capabilities that can deter cyber threats, and we will work with other countries - and the private sector - to protect individuals' data and defend critical infrastructure, including the global financial system."

The differences are subtle, but very real. The GOP, through the lens of *America first* nationalism, looks to partner with its corporations. The Democratic Party, through the lens of world citizenship, looks also to a larger, even a global, community.

Environment and Energy

Energy was a driving consideration for GOP positions. Nowhere was there support for solar or wind power; Republicans unapologetically supported fossil fuels.

> "We support expedited siting processes and the thoughtful expansion of the grid so that consumers and businesses continue to have access to affordable and reliable electricity"

> "Those who mine [coal] and their families should be protected from the Democratic Party's radical anticoal agenda."

> "We intend to finish that [Keystone] pipeline and others as part of our commitment to North American energy security."

> "We support the development of all forms of energy that are marketable in a free economy without subsidies, including coal, oil, natural gas, nuclear power, and hydropower."

> "We respect the states' proven ability to regulate the use of hydraulic fracturing, methane emissions, and horizontal drilling,"

Remarkably, despite unwavering support of fossil fuel in all its forms, the markets have had their way. In June, 2019, the incumbent Republican administration signed a major restructuring of the Clean Power Plan which had been enacted by the Obama Administration. The new rules rolled back limits on the greenhouse gas emissions of coal-fired power plants. Even so, the improving competitiveness of solar and wind generation have canceled out these added subsidies, so the net effect of the rollbacks is to simply allow existing coal plants to operate with more lenient emissions controls. Even so, retirements of US coal plants continued unabated under the GOP administration. [1]

The global oil markets also had their way with the domestic petroleum industry. After decades of subsidies and three years of deregulation, US producers relied on hydraulic fracturing and horizontal drilling - and the *freedom* to dispose of their unwanted methane without unwelcome regulation. The US had become a net exported of oil and gas during the Obama administration, and ramped up its production under the incumbent Republican administration. Fracking and horizontal drilling are expensive extraction methods relative to the producers of Saudi Arabia and elsewhere. A global oil glut that developed leading up to 2019 was resolved by falling prices and squeezed profit margins for US producers. The winners and losers may take years to sort out, but they certainly do not include the domestic oil and gas producers. [2]

The GOP platform clearly favored energy over the environment, and the administration did its best to promote the interests of fossil fuels - remarkably unsuccessfully.

~

Democrats, predictably, embrace the green revolution, even while acknowledging that it requires government subsidies - and the elimination of existing subsidies for fossil fuel miners and drillers. Critically, they also acknowledge the role of the EPA in energy regulation and the need to protect vulnerable environments from extraction.

> "Democrats will immediately rejoin the Paris Climate Agreement and convene a world summit aimed at new and more ambitious global targets to reduce carbon pollution."

> "We will work to ratify the Kigali Amendment to the Montreal Protocol and move expeditiously to phase out super-polluting hydrofluorocarbons in the United States."

> "We will restore funding to the Global Environment Facility and the Intergovernmental Panel on Climate Change, to support critical climate science research around the world."

> "We will support the protection of species and wildlife habitats around the world, including by advancing the goals of

the United Nations Framework Convention on Biological Diversity, and encourage other countries to join us in conserving 30 percent of the planet by 2030."

"Democrats will create an environmental justice fund to make historic investments aimed at eliminating legacy pollution, which disproportionately causes illness and premature death in communities of color, low-income communities, and Indigenous communities."

"We will grow the nation's biofuels manufacturing sector, including by strengthening the Renewable Fuel Standard, supporting E15 blends, and supporting research, development, and deployment of advanced biofuels."

"Democrats commit to eliminating carbon pollution from power plants by 2035 through technology-neutral standards for clean energy and energy efficiency."

"We will dramatically expand solar and wind energy deployment through community-based and utility-scale systems, including in rural areas."

"Within five years, we will install 500 million solar panels, including eight million solar roofs and community solar energy systems, and 60,000 wind turbines, and turn American ingenuity into American jobs by leveraging federal policy to manufacture renewable energy solutions in America."

"We will set a bold, national goal of achieving net-zero greenhouse gas emissions for all new buildings by 2030, on the pathway to creating a 100 percent clean building sector."

"Within five years, we will incentivize tens of billions of dollars in private-sector investment to retrofit four million buildings, including helping local governments save money and cut pollution by weatherizing and upgrading energy systems in hospitals, schools, public housing, and municipal buildings."

Sure, there's a contrast between the parties at the intersection of energy and the environment. It's a contrast that will be vigorously debated wherever energy is created or consumed. And that's pretty much everywhere.

Environment and Public Lands

The Bundy occupations of 2014 and 2016 brought to light a deep division among Americans. Public lands are a common good, but does that good warrant protection against individual or local exploitation? And should that exploitation be viewed positively or negatively? Predictably, the GOP comes down on the side of private landowners and certain users of public lands and water.

> "The EPA's Waters of the United States (WOTUS) rule, issued jointly with the Army Corps of Engineers, is a travesty."

> "…ranching on public lands must be fostered, developed, and encouraged."

> "…we support the opening of public lands and the outer continental shelf to exploration and responsible production, even if these resources will not be immediately developed."

> "Congress shall immediately pass universal legislation providing for a timely and orderly mechanism requiring the federal government to convey certain federally controlled public lands to states"

> "We support amending the Antiquities Act of 1906 to establish Congress' right to approve the designation of national monuments and to further require the approval of the state where a national monument is designated or a national park is proposed."

The incumbent Republican administration has carried through on the actions threatened by the party's platform - and more. Less than a month after inauguration, the administration repealed a rule preventing mining companies from dumping waste into rivers. Officials hostile to the preservation of public lands were appointed and set upon the mission of opening them up to resource extraction for profit. In his first year in power, Trump scaled back National Monuments established by previous administrations, opened Arctic waters for oil drilling, reduced royalties levied against oil and gas extractions, scaled back permitting and environmental review processes for private projects on public lands, proposed new and larger subsidies for coal and nuclear companies, and the following year even pardoned Dwight and

Steven Hammond who had been convicted of arson in connection
with the Malheur Wildlife Refuge seizure.

~

The Democratic worldview is a preservationist one. When the interests of private users of public lands, water, and wildlife come into
conflict with their view of the public good, the public good must
prevail. And the public good includes the public land domain as well
as the air and water in the more broadly defined environment.

> "The Democratic National Committee wishes to acknowledge
> that we gather together to state our values on lands that have
> been stewarded through many centuries by the ancestors and
> descendants of Tribal Nations who have been here since time
> immemorial. We honor the communities native to this
> continent, and recognize that our country was built on
> Indigenous homelands. We pay our respects to the millions of
> Indigenous people throughout history who have protected our
> lands, waters, and animals."

> "We will restore protections for irreplaceable public lands and
> waters, from Bears Ears National Monument to the Arctic
> National Wildlife Refuge. We will follow science and the law
> by reducing harmful methane and carbon pollution from the
> energy sector."

> "We will protect these precious places and preserve America's
> unspoiled wildernesses for hunting, fishing, hiking, and
> camping by codifying the roadless rule, and grow America's
> outdoor recreation economy, which supports millions of jobs
> in rural areas."

> "Democrats will immediately reverse the Trump
> Administration's harmful rollbacks of protections for national
> monuments like Grand Staircase-Escalante National
> Monument and Northeast Canyons and Seamounts Marine
> National Monument."

> "We will take action to protect wildernesses and waters, and
> require full, rigorous, and transparent scientific and
> environmental reviews of any proposed mining projects near
> national treasures."

"We will also support establishment of additional federal co-management agreements with Tribal Nations on federal lands that have cultural and historical significance to Tribes."

"We will hold fossil fuel companies accountable for cleaning up abandoned mine lands, oil and gas wells, and industrial sites, so these facilities no longer pollute local environments and can be safely repurposed to support new economic activity, including in the heart of coal country."

"Democrats will protect wildlife habitats and biodiversity, slow extinction rates, and grow America's natural carbon sinks by conserving 30 percent of our lands and waters by 2030."

There's a contrast, to be sure. Republicans call for the surrender of federal lands to the states, with no provisions to prevent the privatization of that very land. Democrats are willing to continue, through executive order, to create new public domains under the Antiquities Act of 1906.

Health, Research, and Data

Health Care

An ongoing public health crisis is the single most defining difference between the platforms of the parties. A platform written before the Covid-19 pandemic falls woefully short of policy solutions in all three categories of health, research, and data. We have previously examined the response of the incumbent Republican administration to give us some idea of what policies would be implemented in the future.

However, the 2016 GOP platform does offer some general policy planks with regard to health care.

"Any honest agenda for improving health care must start with repeal of the dishonestly named Affordable Care Act of 2010: Obamacare."

"To preserve Medicare and Medicaid, the financing of these important programs must be brought under control before they consume most of the federal budget, including national defense."

"The current federally dictated mental health care regime is wasteful and ineffective, and moving to a block grant approach would allow for state and local governments to create solutions for individuals and families in desperate need of help in addressing mental illness."

"We will not fund or subsidize health care that includes abortion coverage."

"We condemn the Supreme Court's activist decision in Whole Woman's Health v. Hellerstedt striking down commonsense Texas laws providing for basic health and safety standards in abortion clinics."

"We applaud the U.S. House of Representatives for leading the effort to add enforcement to the Born-Alive Infant Protection Act by passing the Born-Alive Abortion Survivors Protection Act, which imposes appropriate civil and criminal penalties on health care providers who fail to provide treatment and care to an infant who survives an abortion....."

"We respect the states' authority and flexibility to exclude abortion providers from federal programs such as Medicaid and other health care and family planning programs so long as they continue to perform or refer for elective abortions or sell the body parts of aborted children."

"Through Obamacare, the current Administration has promoted the notion of abortion as health care. We, however, affirm the dignity of women by protecting the sanctity of human life."

"We oppose school-based clinics that provide referral or counseling for abortion and contraception and believe that federal funds should not be used in mandatory or universal mental health, psychiatric, or socio-emotional screening programs."

"We support state and federal legislation to cap non-economic damages in medical malpractice lawsuits, thereby relieving conscientious providers of burdens that are not rightly theirs and addressing a serious cause of higher medical bills."

The Republican Party, by its own words, is the party of a diminished role of the federal government in public health. Cutting health care starts with the repeal of the Affordable Care Act, then cutting the cost of Medicare and Medicaid to preserve the defense budget, outsourcing Medicaid to the states, and eliminating support for school programs that provide counseling for contraception. An obsessive preoccupation with abortion expresses itself in the withdrawal of federal funding from any entity that even speaks about it. And finally, Republican health care includes protecting health care providers by capping damages awarded to victims of malpractice.

None of these provisions contributed to the capacity of the federal government to respond to the Covid-19 health care crisis; the 2016 Republican platform was of no help at all. And the response of the current Republican administration may have only made matters worse.

~

As we might expect, the Democratic Party takes a more hands-on approach to health care - one intended to address the current crisis. The Party is not unified in its strategic approach to health care reform; the moderate wing promotes the evolution and expansion of the Affordable Care Act to be more inclusive and comprehensive and the progressive wing promotes the implementation of a Medicare program that's made available to all. Although the platform shows that the moderate wing prevails in 2020, the door is left open for future policy shifts.

> "We are proud our party welcomes advocates who want to build on and strengthen the Affordable Care Act and those who support a Medicare for All approach....."

We've seen many of the policy proposals that deal specifically with Covid-19. They include providing free testing, treatment - and when available, vaccines - to every resident. They include the creation of a comprehensive health surveillance program, increased funding for the CDC and state health departments. They even include child care for health care workers and other essential workers and paid sick leave for all workers.

The current pandemic is occurring within an American health care system that was already challenged by inconsistent coverage and rising costs.

"We must guarantee health care not as a privilege for some, but as a right for every single American."

"We will provide direct, increased support to states to enroll eligible adults in Medicaid, have the federal government cover a higher percentage of the bill, and add incentives for states which have not yet expanded Medicaid to do so."

"Democrats will also empower the states, as laboratories of democracy, to use Affordable Care Act innovation waivers to develop locally tailored approaches to health coverage, including by removing barriers to states that seek to experiment with statewide universal health care approaches."

"...we will give all Americans the choice to select a high-quality, affordable public option through the Affordable Care Act marketplace. The public option will provide at least one plan choice without deductibles; will be administered by CMS, not private companies; and will cover all primary care without any co-payments and control costs for other treatments by negotiating prices with doctors and hospitals, just like Medicare does on behalf of older people."

"Democrats support doubling investments in community health centers and rural health clinics, including increased support for dental care, mental health care, and substance use services like medication-assisted treatment, and why we will increase support for mobile health clinics."

"We must also expand funding so state and local public health departments can hire sufficient staff to conduct contact tracing for everyone who tests positive for the novel coronavirus. Only through widespread, regular testing and tracing can we hope to understand the scope of the pandemic and contain it."

"Democrats support making COVID-19 testing, treatment, and any eventual vaccines free to everyone, regardless of their wealth, insurance coverage, or immigration status."

"We will improve oversight and expand protections for residents and staff at nursing homes, which have seen some of the worst COVID-19 outbreaks."

"And we will expand support for telemedicine....."

"...we will outlaw the predatory practice of surprise medical billing."

"We will address the discrimination and barriers that inhibit meaningful access to reproductive health care services, including those based on gender, sexuality, race, income, disability, and other factors."

"We recognize that quality, affordable comprehensive health care, evidence-based sex education, and a full range of family planning services help reduce the number of unintended pregnancies and thereby also reduce the need for abortions."

"We are proud to be the party of the Affordable Care Act, which required insurers to cover prescription contraceptives at no cost to women and has helped significantly reduce teen pregnancy rates."

The Democratic Party's health care strategy continues to rely on insurance companies for payment of medical services, even while offering a public option administered by the Centers for Medicare and Medicaid Services. The public option may develop into an ever larger role over time, but for now *it is not* Medicare for all. And the goal of universal health care for Americans may prove to be elusive.

Research and Data

The Internet and the data it carries are relatively new to party platforms, and join the more traditional policy domains of research and health. Contrasts between the platforms can be seen. The Democratic Party platform deals with medical research in the current context but that context is necessarily lacking in the GOP platform. Republicans cloaked their strategies in free market rhetoric even while mixing a few social issues in for good measure.

Here's what the GOP platform had to say.

"As incubators of unconventional thinking, our country's existing research infrastructure - the National Labs, the National Institutes of Health, NASA, and elements of the Defense Department - have the potential to form partnerships with small businesses to create an American Start-Up Century."

"This [the modern miracle of American medicine] is the consequence of marrying significant investment, both public and private, with the world's best talent, a formula that has for a century given the American people the world's best health care. We are determined that it should continue to do so, especially as we confront new dangers like Ebola, Zika, Chikungunya, and antibiotic-resistant pathogens."

"The FDA needs to return to its traditional emphasis on hard science and approving new breakthrough medicines, rather than divert its attention and consume its resources trying to overregulate electronic health records or vaping."

 "We believe the FDA's approval of Mifeprex, a dangerous abortifacient formerly known as RU-486, threatens women's health….."

"We pledge… that the United States remains the world leader in life sciences and medical innovation, that millions of high-paying, cutting-edge device and drug jobs stay in the United States, that U.S. patients benefit first and most from new devices and drugs, and that the FDA no longer wastes U.S. taxpayer and innovators' resources through bureaucratic red tape and legal uncertainty."

"We urge a ban on human cloning for research or reproduction, and a ban on the creation of, or experimentation on, human embryos for research."

"The internet's free market needs to be free and open to all ideas and competition without the government or service providers picking winners and losers."

 "We call for strong action by Congress and a new [incumbent] Republican president to enforce intellectual property laws against all infringers, whether foreign or domestic."

"We will ensure that personal data receives full constitutional protection from government overreach. The only way to safeguard or improve these systems is through the private sector."

Public-private-partnerships again offered a way for Republicans to outsource government functions to private enterprise while regulating or banning avenues of research repugnant to the Party. We've noted that intellectual property rights accrue primarily to those entities that claim ownership, the overwhelming preponderance of which are commercial corporations. The protection that pharmaceutical companies enjoy often applies to products developed at taxpayer expense. And that protection often is gained at the expense of patients who have contributed their taxes toward the development of the drugs they so desperately need and can ill afford.

The FDA is viewed as an impediment to, rather than a facilitator of effective policy. An institution known for its careful methodology and adherence to precedent ought to be valued by conservatives, but that's not the case here. There's an additional irony in a platform that promotes the *freedom* of the FDA to focus on the approval of submissions and at the same time promotes the *restriction* of its freedom to approve abortifacients such as misoprostol and Cytotec. The influence of the socially conservative evangelical wing of the Party can easily be seen in these planks.

The record of the incumbent Republican administration reflects the 2016 GOP platform. The FDA has been viewed as a rival to the President's authority, and its enforcement actions have been severely curtailed. The exact causes of this decline are unclear, but the issuance of *warning letters* to keep dangerous or ineffective drugs off the market has decline by one-third.

> "Those who think the Trump administration has not succeeded in its deregulatory efforts ought to look at these data," says Peter Lurie, an FDA executive... [3]

Deregulation may be one motivation, but are there other reasons to get the FDA out of the administration's way?

~

The value of a robust federal role in health research is clear in the Democrats' policy statements, but other roles are not neglected. The platform calls for increased funding for research in space, artificial intelligence, energy, and transportation while guarding the intellectual freedom of scientists. Data integrity, universal broadband, and the restoration of net neutrality are strategic concerns exacerbated by current events.

"We will support increased and sustainable funding for health and medical research and federal grants across agencies, including at the National Cancer Institute and other components of the National Institutes of Health (NIH), the CDC, and the Agency for Health Care Research and Quality."

"We will increase the federal investment in research and development for new medications through the NIH, and make sure that there is a return on that investment for taxpayers."

"Democrats will support medical and public health research grants for Historically Black Colleges and Universities (HBCUs) and other Minority-Serving Institutions (MSIs), which are particularly well suited to research health disparities in the context of COVID-19."

"Democrats will support historic federal investments in research, development, demonstration, and deployment, which will break new frontiers of science and create jobs across the country in aerospace, artificial intelligence, advanced materials, biotechnology, and clean energy and clean vehicles."

"Democrats will protect the independence and intellectual freedom of scientists, whether they are employed by the federal government or receiving federal grants in support of their research, and take steps to shield our scientific research agencies from future political interference."

"We will restore funding to the Global Environment Facility and the Intergovernmental Panel on Climate Change, to support critical climate science research around the world."

"Democrats will ensure federal data collection and analysis is adequately funded and designed to allow for disaggregation by race, gender, geography, disability status, and other important variables, so that disparities in health coverage, access, and outcomes can be better understood and addressed."

"Democrats will close the digital divide that deprives more than 20 million Americans of high-speed internet access by investing in broadband and 5G technology, including rural and municipal broadband, and restoring the FCC's authority to take strong enforcement action against internet service providers who violate net neutrality principles."

"...we will work with our allies and partners to develop secure 5G networks [internationally] and address threats in cyberspace."

Read the platforms for yourself and understand how their positions define what and who each of the parties stands for. Science, energy, and the environment, taken together, illustrate the enormous differences between Republicans and Democrats. Each party promotes the interests and protects the rights of a different constituency. To the degree that a platform proves an honest and genuine guide to public policy proposals, we can determine for ourselves if our values and interests are fairly represented by our own party.

SCIENCE, ENERGY, ENVIRONMENT

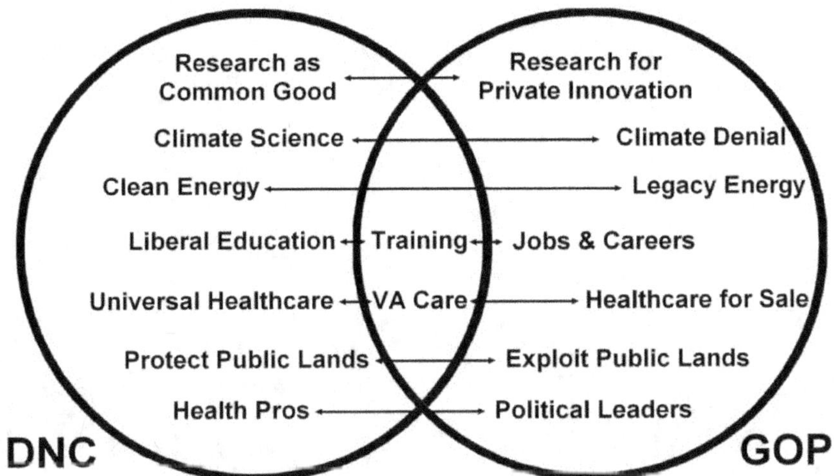

Both Republicans and Democrats believe in science, each party in its own way. The GOP stands ready to subordinate the application of objective science to its ideology and its economic interests. Democrats are more willing to stand back and let scientists and healthcare professionals lead in public policy when they deem it appropriate. The parties agree, however, that job and career training deserves a place in the US educational system, whether or not paid for by the federal government. And everybody agrees that America's military veterans have earned the best care today's medical science can provide.

[1] https://thebreakthrough.org/issues/energy/trumps-war-on-coal

[2] https://blogs.platts.com/2020/06/10/trump-us-oil-diplomacy-executive-orders-producers/

[3] https://www.sciencemag.org/news/2019/07/exclusive-fda-enforcement-actions-plummet-under-trump

Law, Order, and National Security

Make no mistake - there is a difference between the policy platforms of Republicans and Democrats. The issues surrounding law and order, internal security, and the military seem to draw stark contrasts between the positions of the parties. Events following the death of George Floyd show just how different the parties are from each other. The following sections feature direct quotations from each of the platforms, together with a little interpretive commentary.

Land and Order at Home

The GOP saw internal security as a subset of global threats that must be aggressively confronted with tough laws and vigorous enforcement. It assumed that America is presently fearful and unsafe, and that decisive policy action is required to fix it. The right to bear arms was an integral part of the solution to the increased threats represented by the creation of new criminal codes, the public menace of pornography, and a failed immigration system - and confronted by militarized policing and traditional values.

> "We will make America safe."

> "We uphold the right of individuals to keep and bear arms, a natural inalienable right that predates the Constitution and is secured by the Second Amendment."

> "With the murder rate soaring in our great cities, we condemn the Supreme Court's erosion of the right of the people to enact capital punishment in their states."

> "We recommit ourselves, as individuals and as a party, to the rule of law and the pursuit of justice."

> "…we urge caution in the creation of new 'crimes' and a bipartisan presidential commission to purge the Code and the body of regulations of old 'crimes.'"

> "Modifications to [mandatory minimum sentencing] should be
> targeted toward particular categories, especially nonviolent
> offenders and persons with drug, alcohol, or mental health
> issues, and should require disclosure by the courts of any
> judicial departure from the state's sentencing requirements."

> "In solidarity with those who protect us, we call for
> mandatory prison time for all assaults involving serious injury
> to law enforcement officers."

> "Courts should not tie the hands of prison officials in dealing
> with [unruly inmates.]"

Aggressive policing, severe punishments, and unregulated prisons
were seen as an effective way to address crime rates that had been
falling for decades in 2016. Remarkably, the December, 2018 enactment of the First Step Act was an important but modest move
toward criminal justice reform that enjoyed bipartisan support. In
contrast, the administration and its Justice Department moved aggressively to dismantle the federal justice apparatus that had protected
us from political corruption and white collar crime. Republicans often
view *Law and order* on a scorecard of patrols, arrests, convictions, and
imprisonments - especially among those not directly connected to the
Party.

The Republican platform conflated immigration policy with domestic
security and policing, promoting the unsupported notion that un-
documented residents exposed communities to violence and crime.

> "…border security is a national security issue, and that our
> nation's immigration and refugee policies are placing
> Americans at risk."

> "We oppose any form of amnesty for those who, by breaking
> the law, have disadvantaged those who have obeyed it."

> "…unlawful amnesties must be immediately rescinded by a
> Republican president. In a time of terrorism, drug cartels,
> human trafficking, and criminal gangs, the presence of millions
> of unidentified individuals in this country poses grave risks to
> the safety and sovereignty of the United States. Our highest
> priority, therefore, must be to secure our borders and all ports
> of entry and to enforce our immigration laws."

"...we support building a wall along our southern border and protecting all ports of entry."

 "The Department of Homeland Security must use its authority to keep dangerous aliens off our streets and to expedite expulsion of criminal aliens. Gang membership should be a deportable offense."

"Because 'sanctuary cities' violate federal law and endanger their own citizens, they should not be eligible for federal funding."

"We support the right of the states to enact laws deterring illegal aliens from residing within their states."

A policy of *America First* merged with xenophobia in the 2016 GOP platform, and was vigorously pursued in the words and actions of the incumbent Republican administration. Immigration - particularly among those seeking refuge or asylum - was severely restricted. The crime problem so feared by the administration and its supporters expressed itself in internment camps along the border that separated parents from children as a deterrent to those seeking asylum or refugee states.

Ironically, the Christian-evangelical wing - and the conspiracy theory wing - of the Party each had a voice in real or imagined issues that require a public policy response.

"We demand tough penalties against those who engage in identity theft, deal in fraudulent documents, and traffic in human beings."

"Pornography, with its harmful effects, especially on children, has become a public health crisis that is destroying the lives of millions. We encourage states to continue to fight this public menace....."

The GOP platform was mute on the issue of white nationalist terrorist groups and their operations. Such groups were active and growing in 2016, and found allies in the White House after the election. The platform was also mute on demonstrations of civil unrest that the administration subsequently labeled as left-wing terrorist mobs and identified under the nebulous label of *antifa*.

> "The essential role of federal law enforcement personnel in protecting federal property and combating interstate crime should not be compromised by diversion to matters properly handled by state and local authorities."

Remarkably, this plank was abruptly reversed when federal militarized police forces were sent into American cities over the objections of their local authorities to quell peaceful demonstrations and civil unrest. All such cities were administered by governors and mayors identified with the Democratic Party.

~

The Democratic Party platform offers a striking contrast, beginning with an acknowledgment of the failure of the American criminal justice system as it stands today.

> "Our criminal justice system is failing to keep communities safe - and failing to deliver justice. America is the land of the free, and yet more of our people are behind bars, per capita, than anywhere else in the world."

Democrats see criminal justice reform as much more than the increasingly vigorous enforcement of existing laws. At the most fundamental level, Democrats would decriminalize drug use in favor of rehabilitation. They would decriminalize mental health in favor of treatment programs. They would decriminalize poverty and homelessness in favor of equal opportunity.

> "And rather than involving the criminal justice system, Democrats support increased use of drug courts, harm reduction interventions, and treatment diversion programs for those struggling with substance use disorders."

> "All past criminal convictions for cannabis use should be automatically expunged."

> "Poverty is not a crime, and it should not be treated as one. Democrats support eliminating the use of cash bail and believe no one should be imprisoned merely for failing to pay fines or fees. Equal justice under the law should not be contingent on the ability to pay for quality legal representation, which is why we support increasing funding for public defenders and for the Legal Services Corporation."

"Democrats also recognize that all too often, systematic cuts to public services have left police officers on the front lines of responding to social challenges for which they have not been trained, from homelessness to mental health crises to the opioid epidemic."

The platform clearly addresses the increased public awareness of police violence against the very people whose protection is a sworn duty.

"Police brutality is a stain on the soul of our nation."

"Democrats will establish strict national standards governing the use of force, including permitting deadly force only when necessary and a last resort to prevent an imminent threat to life. We will require immediate application of these standards to all federal law enforcement agencies and condition federal grants on their adoption at the state and local level. We will require officer training in effective nonviolent tactics, appropriate use of force, implicit bias, and peer intervention, both at the academy and on the job. And we will ban racial and religious profiling in law enforcement."

"We will collect and publish data on the use of force in police departments across the country to promote transparency and accountability. To increase transparency and improve federal, state, and local law enforcement hiring practices, Democrats will also establish a national registry of officers who have been found to have abused their power."

"Democrats will reinvigorate pattern-or-practice investigations into police misconduct at the Department of Justice, and strengthen them through new subpoena powers and expanded oversight to address systemic misconduct by prosecutors."

"Democrats believe weapons of war have no place on our streets, and will once again limit the sale and transfer of surplus military weapons to domestic law enforcement agencies....."

"We will also act to ensure that victims of federal, state, or local law enforcement abuses of power can seek justice through civil litigation by reining in the doctrine of qualified immunity."

"And we will seek increased funding for officer health and well-being in police departments across the country, including for personal safety equipment and mental health services."

The Democratic Party platform recognizes the reality of race in police violence, and proposes specific policies to address it.

"It is unacceptable that Black parents must have "the talk" with their children, to try to protect them from the very police officers who are supposed to be sworn to protect and serve them. It is unacceptable that more than 1,000 people, a quarter of them Black, have been killed by police every year since 2015."

"We support re-issuing federal guidance from the Department of Education and the Department of Justice to prevent the disparate disciplinary treatment of children of color in school and educational settings."

"Democrats also support measures to increase diversity among the ranks of police departments, so our law enforcement agencies look more like the communities they serve."

"Democrats support lowering the intent standard for federally prosecuting law enforcement officials for civil rights violations."

"We will nominate and confirm federal judges who have diverse backgrounds and experiences, including as public defenders, legal aid attorneys, and civil rights lawyers."

Democrats intend to close private prisons to remove the profit incentive for excessive incarceration. Capital punishment, prisoner rehabilitation, white collar crime, and even *states' rights* make an appearance in the platform. In short, Democrats disagree with Republicans on virtually every aspect of internal security.

"Democrats support ending the use of private prisons and private detention centers, and will take steps to eliminate profiteering from diversion programs, commercial bail, electronic monitoring, prison commissaries, and reentry and treatment programs.”

“Democrats continue to support abolishing the death penalty.”

“Democrats will pursue a holistic approach to rehabilitation, increasing support for programs that provide educational opportunities, including pursuing college degrees, for those in the criminal justice system, both in prison and upon release.”

“...when justified by the law, we will back criminal penalties for reckless executives who illegally gamble with the savings and economic security of their clients and American communities.”

“The Justice Department should not launch federal prosecutions of conduct that is legal at the state level.”

Republicans loudly voice their support for law enforcement institutions and personnel, even having dedicated their platform itself to the cause in the face of widespread abuse. Democrats, even while recognizing the service of law enforcement, call for concrete measures to provide enhanced training and equipment geared toward reinforcing the accountability of policing operations. Going even further, they propose addressing some of the root causes of lawlessness.

Diplomacy and International Law

War has been described as the last option of diplomacy. The parties differ profoundly in their view of how well America’s diplomacy has served its interests in recent years. Diplomatic successes make the threat and reality of war more remote, and diplomatic failures make the threat and reality of war more imminent. Republicans embraced the latter view, citing their perceived failure of American diplomacy.

“Our standing in world affairs has declined significantly - our enemies no longer fear us and our friends no long trust us.”

“All international executive agreements and political arrangements entered into by the current [prior] Administration must be deemed null and void as mere expressions of the current president’s preferences”

"Our continued participation in the United Nations should be contingent upon the enactment of long-overdue changes in the way that institution functions."

"We do not support the U.N. Convention on Women's Rights, the Convention on the Rights of the Child, the Convention on the Rights of Persons with Disabilities, and the U.N. Arms Trade Treaty, as well as various declarations from the U.N. Conference on Environment and Development."

"We should abandon arms control treaties that benefit our adversaries without improving our national security"

"A Republican president will not be bound by [the agreement with Iran.]"

Republicans clearly viewed diplomacy as a sign of national weakness in 2016. The general statements in the platform were converted into specific and decisive action by the incumbent Republican administration. The termination of agreements and commitments seemed to become a point of pride for the President and he tactically withdrew from the world diplomatic stage.

The State of Israel occupied a curious and elevated position in the GOP platform.

"We recognize Jerusalem as the eternal and indivisible capital of the Jewish state and call for the American embassy to be moved there in fulfillment of U.S. law."

"We reject the false notion that Israel is an occupier and specifically recognize that the Boycott, Divestment, and Sanctions Movement (BDS) is anti-Semitic in nature and seeks to destroy Israel."

In May, 2018 the incumbent Republican administration moved the US embassy from Tel Aviv to Jerusalem, thus standing against the United Nations in recognizing the city as the capital of Israel. In June, 2020, with the approval of the President of the United States, Israel approved the development of a Jewish settlement in the occupied Golan Heights. They named it *Trump Heights*. [1]

Although the full measure of its aggression was not widely known when the 2016 GOP platform was written, Russia was nonetheless considered a threat. Its annexation of Crimea and its occupation of parts of Ukraine raised alarms in some quarters of the Party.

> "We support maintaining and, if warranted, increasing sanctions, together with our allies, against Russia unless and until Ukraine's sovereignty and territorial integrity are fully restored"

> "We also support providing appropriate assistance to the armed forces of Ukraine and greater coordination with NATO defense planning."

> "…we demand, as we have in the past, that our fellow members of NATO fulfill their commitments and meet their need for greater investment in their armed forces."

These strong words were sometimes matched by the administration with sanctions against Russian oligarchs and their companies. But the strategic objectives of the Putin government were often advanced, decisively and inexplicably, by the President of the United States. These objectives include: to weaken NATO; to degrade the European Union; to disrupt US leadership in the global economy; to destroy global trust in the US; avoid the consequences of interference in US elections; to destabilize US culture; and to undermine democratic norms and values throughout the world. [2]

~

Democrats embrace a more positive and a broader view of diplomacy and national security. The party found it necessary to restate the fundamentals of diplomacy after the incumbent Republican administration's obliteration of international norms. The platform addresses the issues of climate change leadership, trade agreements, and humanitarian assistance among the diplomatic tools at its disposal, and explicitly acknowledges that war is a last resort.

> "Democrats will lead with diplomacy as our tool of first resort and mobilize our allies and partners to meet the tests none of us can meet on our own."

> "Rather than militarize our foreign policy, treat our diplomats with contempt, and call for reckless budget cuts, Democrats will put diplomacy back in the hands of professionals and ensure they are better prepared to advance American interests

on the central issues of our time, like disruptive technology and climate change."

"Democrats will deliver on this overdue commitment to end the forever wars, and we will do it responsibly - setting priorities, leading with diplomacy, protecting ourselves from terrorist threats, enabling local partners, and bringing our troops home."

"Rather than occupy countries and overthrow regimes to prevent terrorist attacks, Democrats will prioritize more effective and less costly diplomatic, intelligence, and law enforcement tools."

"We will rejoin the Paris Climate Agreement and, on day one, seek higher ambition from nations around the world, putting the United States back in the position of global leadership where we belong."

"Democrats will fully resource the WHO, especially its Contingency Fund for Emergencies, while supporting fundamental reforms and mechanisms to enhance accountability and protect experts from political pressure."

"We will revitalize and expand the Obama-Biden Administration's Global Health Security Agenda, and we will immediately restore the White House National Security Council Directorate for Global Health Security and Biodefense."

"Along with our diplomatic partners, we will incorporate more women into peace processes - where their participation can improve the odds of a peace agreement holding - and ensure women's leadership in peace and security processes globally."

"We will ensure that America's diplomatic and trade agreements include enforcement provisions for workers' rights, and we will fight to end the evils of poverty-wage, child, and slave labor."

"We will combat bribery abroad by expanding on the Foreign Corrupt Practices Act, and we will deploy the full range of America's diplomatic and economic tools to target kleptocrats - including targeted sanctions and visa bans."

"Democrats support a comprehensive diplomatic effort to extend constraints on Iran's nuclear program and address Iran's other threatening activities, including its regional aggression, ballistic missile program, and domestic repression."

"Democrats will restore U.S.-Palestinian diplomatic ties and critical assistance to the Palestinian people in the West Bank and Gaza, consistent with U.S. law."

"We oppose any effort to unfairly single out and delegitimize Israel, including at the United Nations or through the Boycott, Divestment, and Sanctions Movement, while protecting the Constitutional right of our citizens to free speech."

"We will rejoin and reform the WHO, the United Nations Human Rights Council, and the United Nations Population Fund, because in a global public health crisis and a global democratic recession, American leadership is needed more than ever."

"We will reaffirm America's commitment to the United Nations Sustainable Development Goals and promote data efforts and transparency measures that ensure accountability and help identify areas for strategic investment."

Both parties agree on their support for Israel, standing by its expansion of settlements in Palestinian territory. But the contrasts dominate any comparison of platform positions - contrasts that can be explained by each party's view of using military power as a diplomatic tool.

How We Treat Our Military

The parties view American military might very differently. In the years leading up to the 2016 election season, budgetary constraints, together with phased withdrawals from Iraq and Afghanistan, had reduced the sheer size of America's war machine. But the US military was still unrivaled in its size and scope, by far the largest in the world. The GOP platform set out an ambitious framework for increasing its size and scope beyond any recent precedent.

"…the first order of business for a Republican president and Congress will be to restore our nation's military might."

"The men and women of our military remain the world's best. The have been shortchanged in numbers, equipment, and benefits….."

"…we urge Congress to demand the same level of accountability from the Pentagon and the Department of Defense."

"Quite simply, the Republican Party is committed to rebuilding the U.S. military into the strongest on earth, with vast superiority over any other nation or group of nations in the world."

"We must move from a budget-based strategy to one that puts the security of our nation first"

"We need a Reagan-era force that can fight and win two-and one-half wars….."

"We must fund, develop, and deploy a multi-layered missile defense system."

"We must modernize nuclear weapons and their delivery platforms, end the policy of Mutually Assured Destruction, and rebuild relationships with our allies, who understand that as long as the U.S. nuclear arsenal is their shield, they do not need to engage in nuclear proliferation."

"We support lifting the budget cap for defense and reject the efforts of Democrats to hold the military's budget hostage for their domestic agenda."

"More than ever, our government must work with the private sector to advance opportunities and provide assistance to those wounded in spirit as well as in body, whether through experimental efforts like the PAWS (Puppies Assisting Wounded Servicemen) program for service dogs or through the faith-based institutions that have traditionally been providers of counseling and aid."

"We oppose the reinstatement of the draft, except in dire circumstances like world war, whether directly or through compulsory national service."

"We reject the use of the military as a platform for social experimentation and will not accept or continue attempts to undermine military priorities and mission readiness."

"Military readiness should not be sacrificed on the altar of political correctness."

"…[We] will seek fundamental change in the VA's senior leadership structure by placing presidential appointees, rather than careerists, in additional positions of significant responsibility."

"The VA must strengthen and improve its efforts through partnerships with private enterprises….."

Remarkably, the GOP called for releasing the American military machine from budgetary constraints, for an enhanced nuclear weapons strategy, and - *for the first time* - readiness to win "two-and one-half wars."

During the Obama Administration, the Republican Party had actively fostered the myth that the US military was neglected, under-funded, and ill prepared. In 2016 the military budget amounted to $611 billion, or more than 3% of GDP. Adding in the cost of internal security, intelligence, and veterans' care, expenditures approached 5% of GDP. The incumbent Republican administration, together with a captive Congress, increased military spending by $122 billion, or about 20% in the first two years. [3]

Where did the money go? US service personnel numbered 1,455,000 in 2018, an increase of 96,000 over 2016 levels [4]. The budget rose 20% and direct employment rose 7%; the difference was inevitably paid to defense contractors, long a political ally of the GOP.

Even as budgets ratcheted ever higher and personnel were added to the ranks of the services, the US military presence was withdrawn or reduced wherever in the world it might have confronted Russian military forces.

The most fundamental reform was the creation of a *new branch of military service* - The United States Space Force. This was a need that wasn't mentioned in the GOP platform but was an initiative of the incumbent Republican administration. Did this need arise anew during the first three years of the administration? Or were the responsibilities of this branch - developing military space professionals, acquiring military space systems, maturing the military doctrine for space power, and organizing space forces - completely unforeseen by the Party in 2016?

~

Democrats believe in maintaining the unrivaled strength of the US military machine, but they are unwilling to write a blank check. Defense spending sparks a remarkable role reversal in which Democrats become the guardians of the purse strings in defiance of GOP extravagance. But while both parties alike hold those who serve in the highest esteem, Democrats express their reverence in terms of pay, benefits, and restraint in the places and manner of deployment.

Democrats embrace military alliances and are not inclined to act alone with the use of force. They recognize that NATO stands as a bulwark against a common rival - the Russian Federation.

> "Democrats believe our military is - and must be - the most effective fighting force in the world. To keep it that way, we need to bring our forever wars to a responsible end, rationalize our defense budget, invest in the forces and technologies of the future, repair civil-military relations, and strengthen our covenant with service members, veterans, and military families."

> "We can maintain a strong defense and protect our safety and security for less. It's past time to rebalance our investments, improve the efficiency and competitiveness of our defense industrial base, conduct rigorous annual audits of the Pentagon, and end waste and fraud."

> "We will ensure [military] pay and compensation keep pace with the current economy."

> "We will also increase time between deployments, improve educational outcomes for military children, and invest in

career training, education, and entrepreneurship programs for military spouses, who face an unemployment rate twice the national average."

"We will expand tax credits to help family caregivers of our veterans, and ensure they receive the support they need from the VA and Department of Defense."

"We will end the Trump Administration's politicization of the armed forces and distortion of civilian and military roles in decision-making."

"Democrats will hold regular press briefings to explain the legal and policy justifications for military operations....."

"We will work to maintain a strong, credible deterrent while reducing our overreliance and excessive expenditure on nuclear weapons."

"NATO is the world's most formidable military alliance. And together, we stand as champions of universal rights and freedoms around the world."

"We will close the detention center at Guantanamo Bay, enhance transparency, oversight, and accountability in counterterrorism programs and operations, and safeguard civil liberties and the rule of law."

Republicans and Democrats do agree on a few things. American service personnel are revered in politics, as they are in American culture. This reverence is reflected in a commitment to veterans' care and benefits. However, this reverence is expressed differently by the parties. Republicans wanted to toughen up our service by giving them more equipment, doing away with political correctness, keeping women out of combat roles, providing wounded soldiers with puppies, and privatizing the VA. Democrats want to infuse our military with the same human rights they promote for civilians, close Guantánamo, and fully fund the VA.

Ultimately, the differences between the platforms may be better understood by examining a key underlying assumption. Given that the primary external threat to national security is the rise of insurgent terrorism, how shall such insurgencies be addressed? Conventional military operations have proven ineffective in reducing the unrest leading to terrorism, and have even been shown to foster its growth. The dependency of a nation or a political party upon increased militarism to address terrorism requires close scrutiny.

How We Will Use Our Military

Ultimately, military power is created to be used. The GOP claimed the right of America to use its power in accordance with its doctrine of exceptionalism. In a dangerous world, one in which diplomacy has failed, exceptionalism grants us the right - *indeed burdens us with the responsibility* - to use overwhelming military might to wage war.

> "We believe that American exceptionalism - the notion that our ideas and principles as a nation give us a unique place of moral leadership in the world - requires the United States to retake its natural position as leader of the free world."

> "We face a dangerous world, and we believe in a resurgent America."

> "To avoid the overextension of our military, we support a larger active force and oppose the current [prior] Administration's cuts to the National Guard and Reserves."

> "We will meet the return of Russian belligerence with the same resolve that led to the collapse of the Soviet Union."

The incumbent Republican administration has diverted military deployments to the southern border to assist in the construction of its wall and has engaged the US Army Corps of Engineers for the construction of emergency medical facilities and field hospitals in response to the Covid-19 pandemic.

The administration's support for the military has been expressed primarily in terms of spending and speeches. As it has blurred the distinction between foreign threats and civil unrest, it violated traditional norms with the deployment of quasi-military Homeland Security police and Customs & Border Protection officers to the streets of American cities.

Remarkably, the President continues to require the support of the military for such public appearances as his speech at a West Point

graduation ceremony - even after the campus had been cleared due to
the Covid-19 pandemic.

~

The Democratic platform is clear on the subject of military deployment, using as few words as possible. The Party explicitly defers to
Congress to authorize the use of military force. And it vows never to
use American soldiers against peaceful citizens.

> "...we will work with Congress to repeal decades-old
> authorizations for the use of military force and replace them
> with a narrow and specific framework....."
>
> "Democrats will never use active duty soldiers as political
> props, and we will never send military forces to suppress
> Americans exercising their constitutional rights."

Read the platforms for yourself and understand how their positions
define what and who each of the parties stands for. Law, order, and
national security is an aggregation of issues that illustrates the
enormous differences between Republicans and Democrats. Each
party promotes the interests and protects the rights of a different
constituency. To the degree that a platform proves an honest and
genuine guide to public policy proposals, we can determine for ourselves if our values and interests are fairly represented by our own
party.

A surprising degree of harmony can be found between the parties with
respect to law, order, and national security. America's military establishment may not have earned universal respect, but its enlisted service
personnel are universally revered. This respect is extended to military
veterans and the care they receive from the Veterans Administration.

But differences arise in how law and order ought to be maintained
both at home and abroad. Democrats favor addressing lawlessness by
solving its underlying causes and avoiding vigorous enforcement.
Republicans favor the use of force against lawbreakers both domestic
and foreign.

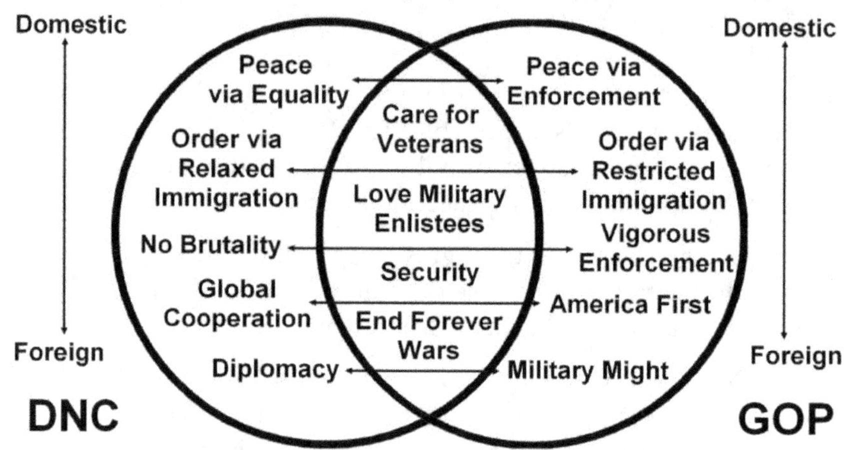

There really is a difference between the parties, but there is some common ground as well. Both parties embrace the values of peace and security. And military service personnel and veterans hold a special place in the American value system as well as the party platforms.

[1] https://www.dw.com/en/israel-approves-trump-heights-settlement/a-53806102

[2] https://themoscowproject.org/reports/putins-payout-10-ways-trump-has-supported-putins-foreign-policy-agenda/

[3] https://www.brookings.edu/research/quality-over-quantity-u-s-military-strategy-and-spending-in-the-trump-years/

[4] https://www.statista.com/statistics/232330/us-military-force-numbers-by-service-branch-and-reserve-component/

Taxes, Spending, and Deficits

Make no mistake - there is a difference between the policy platforms of Republicans and Democrats. The issues surrounding taxes, spending, and deficits reinforce the public image of each party, and confirm the biases that many of us carry with us. By their own words, Republicans were the party of fiscal conservatism; by their own words, Democrats are willing to tax, spend, and borrow for good purposes.

But do the words of the platform really affirm our views of the two parties? And are the actions of the parties consonant with their words? The following sections feature direct quotations from each of the platforms, together with a little interpretive commentary.

Deficits

Deficit spending - the shortfall between the revenues and spending within the annual federal budget - leads to increased debt. As the national debt accumulates year by year and compounds, it becomes a greater burden over time as its interest payments grow. The GOP embraced fiscal responsibility, even while failing to deliver on its promise of balanced budgets.

> "We will fight for Congress to adopt, and for the states to ratify, a Balanced Budget Amendment….."

> "We must impose firm caps on future debt, accelerate the repayment of the trillions we now owe in order to reaffirm our principles of responsible and limited government, and remove the burdens we are placing on future generations."

Remarkably, even when Republicans held the White House and both chambers of Congress, no action was taken with regard to a constitutional amendment to require a balanced budget. Some say that the Party wasn't really serious about the issue. Limits on future debt were likewise discarded on the rubbish heap of political rhetoric.

Subsequent fiscal policy of the incumbent Republican administration ignored the issue of deficits in favor of corporate tax cuts and increased military spending. Immediately before the economic effects of the Covid-19 pandemic, deficits were piling up at a rate of more than $1.1 trillion annually - *during* an economic expansion.

~

While the GOP at least recognized deficits as a problem to be solved, the Democratic Party platform fails to acknowledge the issue with so much as a single mention. Is this a monumental oversight, or does it signal something more profound?

The liberal wing of the Democratic Party has embraced an economic platform that has come to be known as *Modern Monetary Theory - MMT.*

> "Modern Monetary Theory (MMT) is a heterodox macroeconomic theory that, for countries with complete control over their own fiat currency, government spending cannot be thought of like a household budget. Instead of thinking of taxes as income and government spending as expenses in a checkbook, MMT proponents say that fiscal policy is merely a representation of how much money the government is putting into the economy or taking out. In this way, MMT sees fiscal policy in a similar way to how we now think of monetary policy." [1]

If that seems a little technical, it really means that the US government can spend whatever it wants, irrespective of its tax revenues, without significant negative consequences. In effect, *deficits don't matter, and neither does the national debt.*

Conventional economic wisdom says otherwise. Mounting deficits produce one of two consequences - either (1) increases in the supply of money in the economy, or (2) increases in public debt. Increased money supply creates inflation, and public debt may be issued as a way to drain excess money back into the government's balance sheet.

Do deficits and debt matter? We would expect to see much higher levels of inflation in the US economy than are being indicated. But conventional measures of inflation exclude financial assets like US Treasury obligations and the price of shares on stock exchanges. Since most of the increases in money supply are being invested in stocks and bonds, the value of these has soared to record levels.

In effect, the deficits of recent years have served only to inflate stock and bond prices while piling up the debt owed by the federal government to banks, wealthy people, and foreign governments.

This is a monumental failing and a consequence of the incumbent Republican administration's policy of cutting taxes for corporations and increasing military spending. Why doesn't it deserve so much as the tiniest mention? Perhaps it's a concession to the liberal wing, understanding full well that, under the control of the Democratic Party the deficits and resulting debt would look much the same? Perhaps it's a recognition that, once in power, Democrats intend to run up deficits and debts in the same manner, if not for the same purposes.

Tax Increases

The GOP has historically embraced reductions in taxation, regardless of their impact upon deficits or spending on their preferred programs. Even so, they acknowledged that the income tax code is fraught with loopholes that may be unpopular and unproductive - eliminating such loopholes does constitute a de facto tax increase.

> "We will eliminate as many special interest provisions and loopholes as possible and curb corporate welfare, especially where their erosion of the tax base has created pressure for higher rates."

The record of the incumbent Republican administration betrayed the principles stated above. The Tax Cuts and Jobs Act of 2017 further reduced corporate taxes, did little to curb loopholes, and even added complexity to the code. The act also increased personal taxes on balance by eliminating the personal exemption even while doubling the standard deductions, and eliminating or limiting itemized deductions. In the first complete tax year, corporations paid about $91 billion less [2] in income taxes and individuals paid about $90 billion more. [3]

~

Democrats, by contrast, are quite willing to raise taxes. Remarkably, most of the policy statements in their platform relate to corporations, even though corporate taxes fund only about 11% of the federal budget. The rest of the tax increases target the wealthy and highest earners.

> "We will eliminate President Trump's tax and trade policies that encourage big corporations to ship jobs overseas and evade paying their fair share of taxes."

> "If companies shut down their operations here and outsource jobs, we'll claw back any public investments or benefits they received from taxpayers."

> "Democrats will take action to reverse the Trump Administration's tax cuts benefiting the wealthiest Americans and rewarding corporations for shipping American jobs overseas."

> "Corporate tax rates, which were cut sharply by the 2017 Republican tax cut, must be raised, and "trickle-down" tax cuts must be rejected."

> "And we will eliminate tax breaks for prescription drug advertisements."

> "We will make sure investors pay the same tax rates as workers and bring an end to expensive and unproductive tax loopholes, including the carried interest loophole."

> "Estate taxes should also be raised back to the historical norm."

Tax Cuts

Republicans lived up to their reputation by targeting cuts to corporate income tax rates and the rates on income derived from capital rather than labor. They promoted the repeal of Obamacare to cut taxes, but this would have provided meaningful tax relief only to the very highest income taxpayers.

> "Wherever tax rates penalize thrift or discourage investment, they must be lowered. Wherever current provisions of the

code are disincentives for economic growth, they must be changed."

"We propose to level the international playing field by lowering the corporate tax rate to be on a par with, or below, the rates of other industrial nations."

"We need to consider the effect of capital gains rates on the availability of venture capital, as well as the positive impact of expensing on start-up firms."

"The Supreme Court upheld Obamacare based on Congress' power to tax. It is time to repeal Obamacare and give America a much-needed tax cut."

With the exception of repealing Obamacare and the tax surcharges associated with it, these planks were signed into law and implemented. How did that work out?

Remarkably, the added corporate welfare was ineffective in boosting corporate fortunes. In 2018 corporations' savings from the tax cuts was greater than their increase in profits, suggesting that any desired stimulus was in truth merely a transfer payment from individuals to corporations. [4]

The GOP tax cut dogma is based on ideology rather than sound economic principles. The platform's call for greater subsidies for capital investment were seen by the Party as necessary to make domestic corporations competitive on the world stage. Never mind that the ten largest and most successful corporations on the planet were already US corporations.

~

Democrats have historically offered vague, general, expressions of support for "hard working" Americans without any meaningful policy proposals. This platform is different. It proposes tax *cuts* that often take the form of tax credits for specific beneficiaries and purposes rather than changes to the structure of the tax code itself.

"Democrats will reform the tax code to be more progressive and equitable, and reduce barriers for working families to benefit from targeted tax breaks, including the Earned Income Tax Credit and the Child Tax Credit."

"Democrats will make major investments in quality, affordable child care, including by significantly increasing the Child and Dependent Care Tax Credit....."

"We will expand effective tax credits that support domestic manufacturing and grow rural manufacturing jobs through investments in bio-based manufacturing."

"We will create a new tax credit of up to $15,000 to help first-time homebuyers, and will make the tax credit refundable and advanceable, so buyers can get assistance at the time of purchase, instead of having to wait until they file their taxes."

"We will expand the Low-Income Housing Tax Credit to incentivize private-sector construction of affordable housing, and make sure urban, suburban, and rural areas all benefit."

"We will make it easier for working families to benefit from targeted tax breaks, including the Earned Income Tax Credit and the Child Tax Credit, which too often go unclaimed by the lowest-income tax filers."

"Democrats will provide substantially higher levels of support for programs and institutions that boost economic development in America's most impoverished communities, including by... expanding and making permanent the New Markets Tax Credit."

"Democrats will equalize the network of retirement savings tax breaks so that working people can build their nest eggs faster....."

"We will also help Americans pay for long-term care by creating a tax credit for informal and family caregivers and increasing the Child and Dependent Care Tax Credit."

"We will expand access to tax-advantaged ABLE savings accounts, which provide people with disabilities a way to pay for disability-related expenses like housing, education, and transportation."

"We will expand tax credits to help family caregivers of our veterans, and ensure they receive the support they need from the VA and Department of Defense."

The Democratic Party platform doesn't promise tax cuts, except for some who might benefit from a more progressive tax rate schedule - and those who receive tax credits that target spending and investment behaviors the Party wishes to encourage. Each step along the way moves the tax code toward a more complex, more incomprehensible place.

Spending Increases

Contrary to its reputation, the GOP proposed significant but poorly-defined spending increases on border security, space, and the military. Remarkably, the party seemed to be explicitly asking for a blank check for the American war machine.

> "We must move from a budget-based [military] strategy to one that puts the security of our nation first….. We support lifting the budget cap for defense….."

> "Congress and the Administration should work together to approve military spending at the level necessary to defend our country."

> "Military families must be assured of the pay, health care, housing, education, and overall support they have earned. In recent years, they have been carrying the burden of budgetary restraint more than any other Americans through cuts in their pay, health benefits, and retirement plans."

> "…we support building a wall along our southern border and protecting all ports of entry. The border wall must cover the entirety of the southern border and must be sufficient to stop both vehicular and pedestrian traffic."

> "To protect our national security interests and foster innovation and competitiveness, we must sustain our preeminence in space by launching more scientific missions, guaranteeing unfettered access, and ensuring that our space-related industries remain a source of scientific leadership and education."

As noted earlier, military spending was ramped up by about 20% in the first years of the incumbent Republican administration. Because calls for increases remain unchanged in the GOP platform, we may conclude that the Party's appetite for a larger military machine remains unappeased.

Construction of a wall along the southern border has consisted mostly of replacing sections that were deemed inadequate. There are indications that the issue itself is more political red meat and boondoggle than policy of substance.

Space initiatives that were begun or expanded during the incumbent Republican administration have met with considerable success, bipartisan support, and public acclaim.

~

The Democrats do not disappoint with their increased spending proposals. They agree with the GOP in one category only - *space exploration* - but the money from their generosity would otherwise end up in different pockets. All of the remaining increased spending is for domestic programs such as health, jobs and small business, technology and infrastructure, education, and housing.

The health of Americans is clearly top-of-mind among Democrats, and the Party is willing to spend money to improve it.

> "We will substantially increase funding for the Centers for Disease Control and Prevention (CDC) and for state and local public health departments, many of which suffered deep budget cuts during the Great Recession and are at risk of further cuts....."

> "Democrats support doubling investments in community health centers and rural health clinics, including increased support for dental care, mental health care, and substance use services like medication-assisted treatment, and why we will increase support for mobile health clinics."

> "We will also invest in training and hiring more mental health providers, substance use disorder counselors, and peer support counselors, including by expanding funding for health clinics, especially in rural areas, and increasing access to these services through Medicaid."

"Democrats will support medical and public health research grants for Historically Black Colleges and Universities (HBCUs) and other Minority-Serving Institutions (MSIs), which are particularly well suited to research health disparities in the context of COVID- 19."

"We will increase the federal investment in research and development for new medications through the NIH....."

"We will surge funding to the Indian Health Service and support investments to help Tribal governments address the economic fallout of the COVID-19 pandemic....."

"Democrats remain committed to ending the HIV/AIDS epidemic, which disproportionately affects communities of color and the LGBTQ+ community, and will support critical investments under the Ryan White HIV/AIDS Program and the Minority HIV/AIDS Fund."

"To save mothers' lives, Democrats will expand postpartum Medicaid coverage to a full year after giving birth, invest in rural maternal health, promote a diverse perinatal workforce, and implement implicit bias training for health professionals."

"We will invest in community health worker care-forces around the nation proven to prevent, manage, and better treat chronic illnesses, and empower first-time mothers with home visiting."

"...we will invest in mental health and suicide prevention services, and work with our military communities to encourage and support those seeking help, connecting them to critical services."

Democrats intend to increase funding for stimulating employment and for promoting the formation of small entrepreneurial businesses. Child care services are seen as an integral component of full employment, for both providers and consumers.

"Democrats will invest in career and technical education and high-quality job training programs with formal worker representation in program development, including pre-apprenticeship opportunities and registered apprenticeships."

"Democrats will provide substantially higher levels of support for programs and institutions that boost economic development in America's most impoverished communities, including by doubling funding for CDFIs, expanding the Community Development Block Grant, increasing the number of Rural Business Investment Companies, and expanding and making permanent the New Markets Tax Credit."

"Democrats will also make long-overdue investments to upgrade and modernize states' unemployment system technology and ensure the Department of Labor conducts strong oversight of state unemployment systems....."

"Democrats will prioritize support for Black entrepreneurs and other entrepreneurs of color, as well as women entrepreneurs, including by expanding funding for Community Development Financial Institutions (CDFIs) and other proven programs that invest in low-income communities and communities of color."

"We will invest in low-income communities, urban and rural areas, and communities of color by strengthening the Community Reinvestment Act....."

"We will significantly boost funding for state small business grant and lending initiatives that generate tens of billions of dollars of private-sector investment, especially for small businesses owned by women and people of color."

"Democrats will make major investments... by boosting funding for grants to states to help low-income and middle-class families afford child care."

"We will make major investments to increase quality options for parents and increase compensation for [child care] providers."

"We will improve compensation and benefits for child care providers and enact universal, high-quality pre-K programs for three- and four-year-olds."

"We will... invest in career training, education, and entrepreneurship programs for military spouses, who face an unemployment rate twice the national average."

Democrats recognize that investments in technology and infrastructure yield returns ranging from economic development, environmental quality, improved security, to improved public health, greater equality, and more.

"We will invest in innovation hubs and government programs to provide small manufacturers with technical and business expertise....."

"Democrats will support historic federal investments in research, development, demonstration, and deployment, which will break new frontiers of science and create jobs across the country in aerospace, artificial intelligence, advanced materials, biotechnology, and clean energy and clean vehicles."

"Democrats will make investments to create millions of family-supporting and union jobs in clean energy generation, energy efficiency, clean transportation, advanced manufacturing, and sustainable agriculture across America."

"Democrats will invest in modernizing our freight infrastructure, including ports, rail, and maritime freight, in order to reduce air and water pollution, improve public health, create jobs, and improve economic competitiveness."

"Democrats stand ready to take immediate, decisive action... by investing in infrastructure, care work, clean energy, and small businesses to put Americans to work in good-paying jobs; shoring up state and local budgets to save jobs and protect public health in the ongoing COVID-19 pandemic....."

"We will launch our country's second great railroad revolution by investing in high-speed rail, and commit to public transportation as a public good, including ensuring transit jobs are good jobs."

"Democrats will upgrade our nation's ports, lock and dam systems, and freight infrastructure to accommodate 21st century cargo, reduce air and water pollution, and create and maintain high-quality, good-paying jobs."

"We will build a modern electric grid by investing in interstate transmission projects and advanced, 21st century grid technologies to power communities with clean electricity....."

"We will repair, modernize, and expand our highways, roads, bridges, and airports, including by installing 500,000 public charging stations for electric vehicles, ensuring our passenger transportation systems are resilient to the impacts of climate change, and using safe, modern design approaches that allow drivers, pedestrians, cyclists, and others to safely share the road."

"We will increase investment in innovative water technologies, including water use efficiency, water conservation, and water reuse and recycling, that reduce water waste and consumer bills."

"We will invest in technology and forces that meet the threats of the future - from cyber to space, and artificial intelligence to unmanned systems - and reinforce the alliances and partnerships that enhance our collective security."

"We will increase public investment in rural, urban, and Tribal broadband infrastructure and offer low-income Americans subsidies for accessing high-speed internet, so children and families can fully participate in school, work, and life from their homes."

"Democrats will close the digital divide that deprives more than 20 million Americans of high-speed internet access by investing in broadband and 5G technology, including rural and municipal broadband....."

"We will increase investments in public transportation, understanding that the United States currently lags behind many other developed countries in the quality and availability of efficient and accessible public transportation."

Democrats believe that a well educated America is a better America, and they are willing to spend money to make it so.

"We will increase investments in high-quality science, technology, engineering, and mathematics programs in our public schools, support access to computer science for all and improve professional development opportunities for math and science teachers, including through the creation of a national science corps of outstanding STEM teachers serving as leaders in their schools and communities."

"Democrats will extend significant aid to state and local governments, school districts, and public and nonprofit colleges and universities, including HBCUs and MSIs, to address these budget shortfalls and secure jobs."

"We believe in the value of lifelong learning, and will increase investments to support adult literacy and other skills development programs."

"We believe education is a critical public good, and will increase investments to guarantee all students can access high-quality public schools, no matter where they live."

"We will modernize and green our public schools, and ensure they are accessible to students with disabilities."

"We will need increased investments in public education to help students get back on track when public health experts determine it is safe to return to schools."

"Democrats will significantly expand funding for the Bureau of Indian Education and invest in improving public school buildings."

Housing is seen as a continuing need that must be addressed in public policy.

"We will increase investments in public housing to expand availability for the first time since the 1990s, and improve and upgrade existing public housing to ensure safe living conditions for residents, protecting tenants' rights to return if extensive renovations are needed."

"Democrats will supercharge investment in the Housing Trust Fund to greatly expand the number of affordable, accessible housing units on the market."

"Democrats will substantially increase investments to meet Tribal housing needs, including by constructing and upgrading affordable housing on Tribal lands, investing in drinking and clean water infrastructure, and investing in rural and Tribal broadband infrastructure."

Other categories of spending do not escape the attention of Democratic Party policymakers. In their own words, "Whether it's health care, the economy, education, gun reform, equal pay, voting rights, national security, or the climate crisis, the Democratic Party understands that there's no single issue that matters more than the rest. Democrats are tackling these issues and others every day." [5] In effect, *everything counts.*

> "Democrats are committed to pursuing environmental justice and climate justice, including for Indigenous peoples and communities, and will invest significant new resources in clean water and wastewater infrastructure, clean energy generation and distribution, and sustainable and regenerative agriculture."

> "Democrats will increase investments to help state and local governments upgrade election technology, including cybersecurity technology, and ensure that election technology is accessible for people with disabilities."

> "We will invest in [Puerto Rico's] future through economic development initiatives, increased education funding, construction of affordable housing, and innovative energy and climate resilience programs."

> "Democrats will support investments to help the U.S. territories recover from recent natural disasters and build increased resilience to the impacts of climate change, including by expanding access to clean, affordable, reliable energy and water systems."

> "Democrats will prioritize investments in more effective and cost-efficient community-based alternatives to detention [of immigrants]."

> "Democrats will support and invest in long overdue reforms to make the State Department more strategic, modern, agile, and effective."

Spending Cuts

The GOP called for cuts in farm programs, Medicare, Medicaid, education - and implicitly, Social Security. These are the very programs Democrats want to bolster.

> "…spending restraint is a necessary component that must be vigorously pursued"

> "Federal programs to assist farmers in managing risk must be as cost-effective as they are functional, offering tools that can improve producers' ability to operate when times are tough while remaining affordable to the taxpayers."

> "Of the many reforms being proposed, all options should be considered to preserve Social Security. As Republicans, we oppose tax increases and believe in the power of markets to create wealth....."

> "Without disadvantaging present retirees or those nearing retirement, set a more realistic age for [Medicare] eligibility in light of today's longer life span."

> "[Medicaid] is the next frontier of welfare reform. It is simply too big and too flawed to be administered from Washington."

> "…the Constitution gives [the federal government] no role in education….. Of that amount [devoted to K-12 education in 2011-2012,] federal spending amounted to more than $57 billion."

The GOP is the party of fiscal restraint, but when its constituency needs help, it's quick to open the country's checkbook. Following the incumbent Republican administration's trade wars, farm subsidies were *increased* to the highest levels in fourteen years. [6]

Although the GOP called for saving Social Security, it was unwilling to touch the "third rail" with specifics. Such specifics that Republicans are likely to propose would certainly involve reductions in benefits. However, since funding for Social Security is deposited into the OASI trust fund, it cannot be used to offset increased spending in other categories.

Medicare and Medicaid were clearly in the crosshairs of GOP spending hawks four years ago, and remain so today. Although both programs have served their participants well during the Covid-19 pandemic, the Party continues to call for limiting, rather than expanding, Medicare eligibility. Calls continue for Medicaid to be removed from federal jurisdiction, given to states, and funded by block grants.

Understandably, public education was a target for spending cuts in 2016. The incumbent Republican administration has taken every opportunity to undermine it with the appointment of its enemies to the Department of Education, with the diversion of support from public schools to private schools - and outright spending cuts. The President's budget request of 2017 (Obama Administration) was $79.5 billion. The President's budget request of 2019 was $65.8 billion, [7] much of which had been diverted to parochial schools.

Does the US Constitution give the federal government a role in education? These are among its first words.

> "We the People of the United States, in Order to... promote the general Welfare, and secure the Blessings of Liberty to ourselves and our Posterity....."

~

Only one category of federal spending is in the crosshairs of the Democratic Party.

> "Democrats believe the measure of our security is not how much we spend on defense, but how we spend our defense dollars and in what proportion to other tools in our foreign policy toolbox and other urgent domestic investments. We believe we can and must ensure our security while restoring stability, predictability, and fiscal discipline in defense spending. We spend 13 times more on the military than we do on diplomacy. We spend five times more in Afghanistan each year than we do on global public health and preventing the next pandemic. We can maintain a strong defense and protect our safety and security for less. It's past time to rebalance our investments, improve the efficiency and competitiveness of our defense industrial base, conduct rigorous annual audits of the Pentagon, and end waste and fraud."

Although the Democratic Party platform refers to cost saving by implementing efficiency measures, it makes no pretense of directly reducing expenditures at all. The party's financial vision consists of taxing, borrowing - and spending the proceeds.

Rearranging the Deck Chairs

Not every change in taxation or spending affects budget deficits or the national debt. In some cases, policy statements serve to protect the status quo. In other cases, revenue sources are swapped out for others of the same magnitude. In still other cases - as in block granting to states - one type of expenditure is swapped out for another of the same magnitude. Consider the GOP's 2016 positions.

> "Because of the vital role of religious organizations, charities, and fraternal benevolent societies in fostering generosity and patriotism, they should not be subject to taxation and donations to them should remain deductible."

> "…any value added tax or national sales tax must be tied to the simultaneous repeal of the Sixteenth Amendment, which established the federal income tax."

> "We propose to remove from the Highway Trust Fund programs that should not be the business of the federal government."

> "With Republican leadership, the House of Representatives has passed legislation to set up just such a commission [to convert to a gold standard.] We recommend its enactment by the full Congress and the commission's careful consideration of ways to secure the integrity of our currency."

> "Give others [under age 55] the option of traditional Medicare or transition to a premium-support model….."

> "We will give [states] a free hand to [modernize Medicaid] by block-granting the program without strings."

> "As Republicans, we oppose tax increases and believe in the power of markets to create wealth and to help secure the future of our Social Security system."

The incumbent Republican administration has taken certain actions with regard to some of these planks. In May, 2017 the President signed an executive order [8] limiting federal enforcement against churches of the *Johnson Amendment* - which prohibits organizations that are exempt under section 501(c)(3) of the Internal Revenue Code from engaging in political campaign activities.

The Tax Cuts and Jobs Act of 2017 substantially reduced corporate income taxes, but also *raised* personal income taxes for many Americans. The Republican House, Senate, and Administration were not consistent in their compliance with the Republican Party platform.

The remaining issues were largely ignored or flagrantly flouted by the administration.

~

The Democratic Party platform does not directly address spending or revenue offsets. At the most fundamental level, the spending pro-posals fall into one of two categories.

The first includes expenditures that displace or eliminate costs that are now borne by individuals and paid for out of their own pockets. Such expenditures would include the establishment of rural health centers and clinics offering no-cost or low-cost services to the underprivileged, and grants to states to provide subsidized child care services. The costs are transferred from individuals and families to the federal government.

The second spending category includes investments in projects and programs that yield value over time in excess of the money invested. Such investments would include technical education and job training programs that raise tax revenues through higher compensation in the future, and direct support of federal research and development that fosters innovation and economic growth.

Read the platforms for yourself and understand how their positions define what and who each of the parties stands for. Taxes, spending, and deficits is an aggregation of issues that illustrates the enormous differences between Republicans and Democrats. Each party pro-motes the interests and protects the rights of a different constituency. To the degree that a platform proves an honest and genuine guide to public policy proposals - and that may not always be the case - we can determine for ourselves if our values and interests are fairly represented by our own party.

The platforms of the parties confirm the stereotypes we hold - Democrats are spendthrifts and Republicans are tightwads. And there are no surprises to be found. However, the incumbent Republican administration has revealed a glaring hypocrisy in its willingness to run enormous deficits, even during an economic expansion, in order to achieve its promise of corporate tax cuts. The following diagram illustrates the most fundamental differences in the fiscal policies between the parties - as well as a surprising agreement with respect to deficits and cuts in personal income taxes.

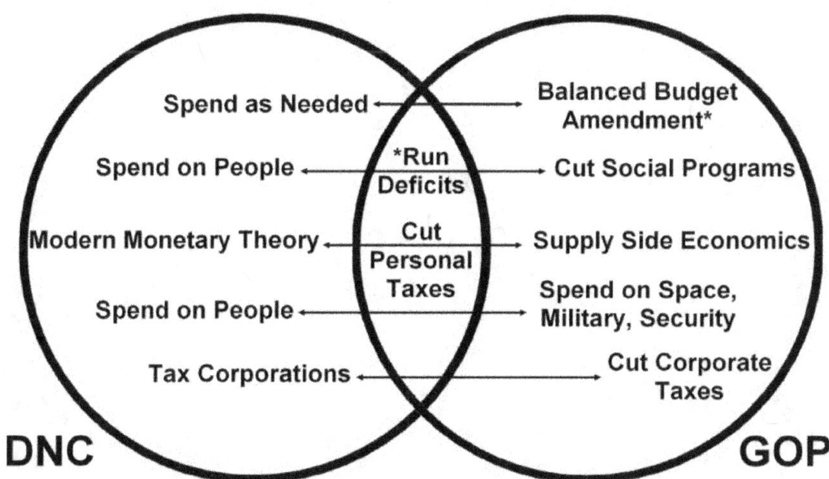

There are some stark contrasts here, as expected. But the parties stand shoulder to shoulder when they find it to their advantage to run up fiscal deficits even while embracing the value of fiscal responsibility.

[1] https://www.investopedia.com/modern-monetary-theory-mmt-4588060

[2] https://finance.yahoo.com/news/corporations-paid-91-billion-less-in-taxes-in-2018-under-trumps-tax-law-160745447.html

[3] https://finance.yahoo.com/news/american-taxpayers-paid-nearly-100-billion-more-to-irs-under-trump-tax-law-194900782.html

[4] https://www.opednews.com/articles/Trump-s-Economy--It-s-a-F-by-Larry-Butler-Corporations_Economy_Economy-Recession_Economy-Economics--US-200124-178.html

[5] https://democrats.org/where-we-stand/

[6] https://www.npr.org/sections/thesalt/2019/12/31/790261705/farmers-got-billions-from-taxpayers-in-2019-and-hardly-anyone-objected

[7] https://www2.ed.gov/about/overview/budget/history/index.html

[8] https://www.natlawreview.com/article/president-trump-signs-johnson-amendment-executive-order-limiting-treasury-s-actions

Omissions, Contradictions, Distortions, and Lies

Make no mistake - there is a difference between the policy platforms of Republicans and Democrats. Each platform presents itself and its party in such a way as to promote its own interests, and at times the truth is subordinated to those interests.

Each of the candidates has offered his or her commentary on their own policies, as well as the policies of the other party and the statements of the other candidate. Contradictions, distortions, and lies can be detected in much of this commentary, but is well beyond the scope of this chapter. Today's lie detectors include www.snopes,com, http://www.factcheck.org, http://www.politifact.com, http://mythopedia.mediamatters.org, http://maplight.org, http://www.prwatch.org, https://www.truthorfiction.com, http://webskeptic.wikidot.com, and specialized sites like http://vmyths.com, http://www.wolframalpha.com, http://www.opensecrets.org, http://www.charitynavigator.org, and others. Each is a valuable resource in its own way.

So we'll leave the candidates' lies to the professionals - this chapter is long enough anyway - and we'll look primarily at the platforms to interpret this issue. In a few places we'll refer to founding documents, other external authorities, and even the Bible to illuminate the veracity of the platforms. In other places quotations will stand alone, allowing the reader to discern the truth or fiction of each. The following sections feature direct quotations from each of the platforms, together with a little interpretive commentary.

Well, okay - you'll find *a little more* interpretive commentary than in previous chapters. You may detect more of my own bias showing through, and I hope you do. For that I do not apologize. If you have a problem with that, get your own copy of the Constitution, the Declaration of Independence, and each of the platforms - then write your own book with your own biases.

Omissions

The most glaring omission, of course, is the total absence of a Republican Party platform for 2020. *Most outrageously,* the most urgent of today's public policy issues have developed *during* the incumbent Republican administration. A four-year old platform cannot begin to address these issues.

By failing to publish a platform, the Republican Party effectively ignores the most critical public health crisis in a century. The Party ignores Russian interference in the 2016 election and continuing efforts to support GOP candidates and causes by means both legal and illegal. The Party ignores public outrage directed at a continuing policy of family separation and the incarceration of children along the southern border of the US. The Party ignores the unprecedented unabashed corruption throughout the executive branch of its incumbent Republican administration. And the Party ignores the deployment of militarized federal police forces to the streets of American cities to confront demonstrators exercising their First Amendment rights of speech and assembly.

That the Republican Party chooses to hide from the realities and consequences of its own policies is understandable; but it is no less inexcusable.

~

The Democratic Party platform, at 80 pages, is much longer than the 2016 GOP platform, and quite comprehensive. It deals with every broad category of the opposition with a level of detail that is at times excruciating.

Even so, it was mute on at least one very important issue. Many Americans are concerned about federal deficits, and a national debt that has risen to alarming levels and beyond. Tacitly embracing a fringe economic school of thought - *Modern Monetary Theory* - as an excuse for failing to address the issue is comparable to the Republicans embracing their own fringe economic school - *Supply Side* - as an excuse to cut corporate taxes. Democrats have shown us how they intend to reform taxes and they have shown us how they intend to increase spending. But they have not shown us how they will pay for any of it - and Americans want to know.

The Democratic Party also ignores a few issues that may be important to certain segments of the American populace, including the widespread religious persecution of American Christians. It barely mentions the scourge of child sex predation among Democratic leaders. It fails to deal with the issue of abortion-as-murder and the sale of body parts by abortion providers. And it completely ignores a weakened military that remains vulnerable to our foes both at home and abroad.

And there's not a word about Democrats' appetite for eating their young.

Contradictions

The following quotations came from the 2016 Republican Party platform. In some cases quotes may be paired to illustrate internal contradictions. In other cases, external sources may be quoted to illuminate inconsistencies, or merely referenced in commentary.

Law and Criminal Justice

> "We are the party of the Declaration of Independence and the Constitution."

Remarkably, the party of the Constitution explicitly subordinated its authority to that of sacred law.

> "…if God-given, natural, inalienable rights come in conflict with government, court, or human-granted rights, God-given, natural, inalienable rights always prevail….."

The GOP, by its own words, is the party of the Bible, not the Constitution.

> "The constitutionality of the death penalty is firmly settled by its explicit mention in the Fifth Amendment."

The fifth Amendment actually says this: "No person shall be held to answer for a capital, or otherwise infamous crime, unless on a presentment or indictment of a Grand Jury, except in cases arising in the land or naval forces, or in the Militia, when in actual service in time of War or public danger; nor shall any person be subject for the same offence to be twice put in jeopardy of life or limb; nor shall be compelled in any criminal case to be a witness against himself, nor be deprived of life, liberty, or property, without due process of law; nor shall private property be taken for public use, without just compensation."

> "...we urge caution in the creation of new "crimes" and a bipartisan presidential commission to purge the Code and the body of regulations of old 'crimes.'"

Within their own platform were calls for additional legislation, some of which is unprecedented in its scope of control.

> "In solidarity with those who protect us, we call for mandatory prison time for all assaults involving serious injury to law enforcement officers." "Pornography, with its harmful effects, especially on children, has become a public health crisis that is destroying the lives of millions. We encourage states to continue to fight this public menace....." "We salute the many states that now protect women and girls through laws requiring informed consent, parental consent, waiting periods, and clinic regulation." "...we support legislation to require proof of citizenship when registering to vote and secure photo ID when voting." "Our laws and our government's regulations should recognize marriage as the union of one man and one woman and actively promote married family life as the basis of a stable and prosperous society."

> "We uphold the right of individuals to keep and bear arms, a natural inalienable right that predates the Constitution and is secured by the Second Amendment."

Recognizing that the GOP is the party of originalist interpretation, the Second Amendment's words are as follows. "A well regulated Militia, being necessary to the security of a free State, the right of the people to keep and bear Arms, shall not be infringed." It's clear that the framers were referring to weapons of war in the hands of an organized band loyal to and controlled by the President of the United States. Originalism requires that every citizen be permitted to have access to such weapons, regardless of their lethality, provided that they are in an organized militia loyal to the President. But is it an inalienable right that predates the Constitution?

"Accordingly, we assert the sanctity of human life and affirm that the unborn child has a fundamental right to life which cannot be infringed."

And yet, the GOP affirmed,

"We support a constitutional amendment to protect [a parent's right to determine a child's care] from interference by states, the federal government, or international bodies such as the United Nations."

Who has authority over a child in a womb - the parent or the government?

Jobs and the Economy

"Pundits and Democrats tell us that we should accept the new normal of a slow-growing economy."

The Democratic Party platform actually says this: "Democrats believe we can spur more sustainable economic growth, which will create good-paying jobs and raise wages."

"The greatest asset of the American economy is the hard-working American. That is why our first priority is getting people back to work by fostering the kind of growth that creates jobs."

Elsewhere in the GOP platform it flatly stated,

"In the face of these [national security] threats, the first order of business for a Republican president and Congress will be to restore our nation's military might."

What came first?

"All Americans deserve the opportunity to pursue their American dream free from discrimination. Clear non-discrimination policies ensure all employees have the chance to succeed based solely on their merits." "…we reject unfair preferences, quotas, and set-asides as forms of discrimination."

Discrimination, however benign, was promoted elsewhere in the platform.

> "We will retain the preference given to veterans when they seek federal employment."

Can we have it both ways?

> "We reject the old maxim that Social Security is the 'Third Rail' of American politics, deadly for anyone who would change it."

Although they may reject the maxim, the party failed to deal with the issue in its 2016 platform, merely stating that all options should be explored.

> "The Democratic Party still treats [Social Security as the 'third rail' of American politics], even though everyone knows that its current course will lead to a financial and social disaster."

The 2016 Democratic Party platform actually addresses the issue with specific policy statements. "Democrats will expand Social Security so that every American can retire with dignity and respect, including women who are widowed or took time out of the workforce to care for their children, aging parents, or ailing family members. The Democratic Party recognizes that the way Social Security cost-of-living adjustments are calculated may not always reflect the spending patterns of seniors, particularly the disproportionate amount they spend on health care expenses. We are committed to exploring alternatives that could better and more equitably serve seniors. We will make sure Social Security's guaranteed benefits continue for generations to come by asking those at the top to pay more, and will achieve this goal by taxing some of the income of people above $250,000. The Democratic Party is also committed to providing all necessary financial support for the Social Security Administration so that it can provide timely benefits and high-quality service for those it serves."

While the 2016 Democratic platform was the subject of the Republican contradiction, it does ring a little truer with respect to the 2020 Democratic platform. "We will enact policies to make Social Security more progressive, including increasing benefits for all beneficiaries, meaningfully increasing minimum benefit payments, increasing benefits for long duration beneficiaries, and protecting surviving spouses from benefit cuts. We will eliminate penalties that unfairly reduce public sector workers' earned Social Security benefits. In light of weakened retirement security for unpaid caregivers and caregivers for family members, who sacrifice not only wages but Social Security benefits when they swap paid labor for unpaid care work, Democrats support Social Security reform which better accounts for the challenges facing unpaid caregivers—including incremental reforms to the benefit formula to mitigate the penalty for unpaid care. Democrats will reject every effort to cut, privatize, or weaken Social Security, including attempts to raise the retirement age, diminish benefits by cutting cost-of-living adjustments, or reduce earned benefits. We will ensure Social Security will be there forever."

Science, Climate, Energy, and Medicine

"Information concerning a changing climate, especially projections into the long-range future, must be based on dispassionate analysis of hard data."

Really, GOP?

"The FDA needs to return to its traditional emphasis on hard science and approving new breakthrough medicines….."

But the GOP backtracked when the FDA uses its hard science to approve things they don't like.

"We believe the FDA's approval of Mifeprex, a dangerous abortifacient formerly known as RU-486, threatens women's health, as does the agency's endorsement of over-the-counter sales of powerful contraceptives….."

"We support the development of all forms of energy that are marketable in a free economy without subsidies, including coal, oil, natural gas, nuclear power, and hydropower."

The contradiction here lies in the existing federal subsidies for coal, oil, natural gas, and hydropower that were expanded, and the regulations that were eased and suspended by the incumbent Republican Administration.

Civil Rights and Society

"We pledge to protect the voting rights of every citizen….."

Fully knowing the insignificance of voter fraud in American, and fully knowing the practical techniques for curtailing voting rights demographic by demographic, the GOP flatly stated,

> "We are concerned, however, that some voting procedures
> may be open to abuse. For this reason, we support legislation
> to require proof of citizenship when registering to vote and
> secure photo ID when voting."

> "All Americans deserve the opportunity to pursue their
> American dream free from discrimination. Clear
> nondiscrimination policies ensure all employees have the
> chance to succeed based solely on their merits." "…we reject
> unfair preferences, quotas, and set-asides as forms of
> discrimination."

Discrimination, however benign, was promoted elsewhere in the
platform.

> "We will retain the preference given to veterans when they
> seek federal employment."

Can we have it both ways?

> "We are the party of independent individuals and the
> institutions they create together — families, schools,
> congregations, neighborhoods - to advance their ideals and
> make real their dreams."

Independent individuals must be free to choose the form and makeup
of their family; and yet the GOP proposed to favor one particular
form.

> "Conversely, as we have learned over the last five decades, the
> loss of faith and family life leads to greater dependence upon
> government." "We oppose policies and laws that create a
> financial incentive for or encourage cohabitation." "The data
> and the facts lead to an inescapable conclusion: Every child
> deserves a married mom and dad."

~

The Democratic Party platform reflects a good deal more care in its
composition than did the 2016 GOP platform. Even so, a few internal
contradictions can be found here as well, but they are far more subtle.

> "We recognize that the official poverty rate, as measured and
> communicated by the federal government, fails to capture
> critical needs like housing, education, health care, trans-

portation, energy, and other necessities, and therefore
understates the true share of Americans living in poverty."

The poverty rate is a logical construct with established and long-used metrics. The *true share of Americans living in poverty* is a subjective concept. The contradiction lies in the illogical contrast between the metric and a nebulous *true rate*.

"America is the land of the free, and yet more of our people
are behind bars, per capita, than anywhere else in the world."

This one isn't subtle at all; the land of the free wouldn't lead the world in incarceration.

"We will ensure Social Security will be there forever."

The contradiction here lies in the total absence of platform planks or policy proposals to ensure the future of Social Security. Current policy requires that benefits be paid out of the Social Security trust fund - the OASI. The OASI will be exhausted in fourteen years - even sooner if the reforms proposed elsewhere in the platform are implemented. When the trust fund runs dry, benefits will be cut back to the level of contributions to the fund from payroll taxes. Some estimate benefit reductions of up to 40% at that time, with additional cuts to follow. Remarkably, the 2016 Democratic Party platform proposed a solution by revising the earnings cap on payroll taxes.

Distortions

Many of the distortions in the parties' platforms originate in their characterization of the other party's beliefs or positions. Such distortions are often the converse of the legal concept of puffery - exaggerated or false praise. The GOP freely indulges in the straw man fallacy, which unfairly characterizes the other party or their position. One of the reasons that there are so many examples of GOP deception is their preoccupation with the previously incumbent party. Overstating the shortcomings of the opposition is only effective when the opposition is the party of incumbency and the loyal opposition can be expected to indulge in the practice. This is just one of the many ironies of the recycling of the 2016 Republican Party platform.

Law and Criminal Justice

"…the Attorney General's present campaign of harassment against police forces around the country….."

"…the next president must not sow seeds of division and distrust between the police and the people they have sworn to serve and protect."

In 2014, the Obama Administration offered assistance to state, county, and municipal law enforcement in their police reform efforts. Assistance ranged from funding for body cameras to investigative resources, to training in best practices for community policing. Attorney General Holder (referenced above) viewed killings by police officers as a problem worth addressing. The 2016 GOP platform characterized these initiatives as *harassment*.

Science, Climate, Energy, and Medicine

"The Democratic Party does not understand that coal is an abundant, clean, affordable, reliable domestic energy resource."

"The Democratic Party's campaign to smother the U.S. energy industry takes many forms…"

"They have directly attacked the production of American energy and the industry-related jobs that have sustained families and communities."

"The taxpayers will not soon forget the current [prior] Administration's subsidies to companies that went bankrupt without producing a kilowatt of energy." "Who will remind us of the 27 fossil fuel companies - all of which enjoyed federal subsidies - that have declared bankruptcy in the first four months of 2016?"

"The [previous] President and the Democratic party have dismantled Americans' system of health care."

Providing public subsidies to nascent industries is a widely-accepted and long-practiced public policy, and some individual failures are to be expected. If the people won't forget the failures occurring during previous administrations, it'll be because the GOP keeps reminding them. [1]

Republicans will always remind us how Democrats have failed to bring affordable health care to the American people; but claiming that they have ever dismantled *anything* is an egregious distortion.

Jobs and the Economy

"Under President Obama and the Democrats, new private-sector jobs are three million below where they should have been with just average modern post-recession growth."

"This is the progressive pathology: Keeping people dependent so that government can redistribute income."

"They [the previous President and the Democratic Party] have nearly doubled the size of the national debt."

"The [previous] President has been regulating to death a free market economy that he does not like and does not understand. He defies the laws of the United States by refusing to enforce those with which he does not agree. And he appoints judges who legislate from the bench rather than apply the law."

"Determined to crush the double-digit inflation that was part of the Carter Administration's economic legacy..."

Two oil shocks, three rounds of wage-price controls, and a draconian monetary policy predated the Carter Administration.

"The Democrats play politics with farm security."

The 2016 GOP platform featured a narrative that the economic growth record of the previous administration could have been better. Their narrative was and is based upon the notion that supply-side corporate tax cuts would have spurred even better growth. The actual economists, even within the Party, know better. Growth may be stimulated by trickle-down policies, but as recent economic history has shown, such growth is quite unsustainable. [2]

Republicans accused Democrats of deliberately exploitative policies solely to promote their Party's interests. They also laid the responsibility for the national debt at the feet of the opposition. They accused the previous administration of economic ignorance and defiance of law. Where is the truth in these planks?

Farm security involves subsidies for agribusiness and food stamps - loosely associated policy realms that have been bound together for decades. GOP conservatives attempted to gut food stamps in the 2014 farm legislation, while leaving corporate subsidies intact. The GOP refers to the Democrats' resistance to this effort as playing politics. [3]

Civil Rights and Society

> "They refuse to control our borders but try to control our schools, farms, businesses, and even our religious institutions."

> "We oppose tax policies that deliberately divide Americans or promote class warfare."

> "Instead of facilitating change, the current [prior] Administration and its agents at the National Labor Relations Board are determined to reverse it."

If Democrats were trying to exert control over schools, farms, businesses, and churches by promoting class warfare and reversing the progress of labor, it certainly reflects a party that lacks any semblance of purpose or strategy. No evidence is offered for these absurd charges.

Immigration, Diplomacy, and International Relations

> "With all our fellow citizens, we have watched, in anger and disgust, the mocking of our immigration laws by a president who made himself superior to the will of the nation."

> "Our standing in world affairs has declined significantly - our enemies no longer fear us and our friends no long trust us."

> "The leadership of the Democratic Party, both those in office and those who seek it, no longer see America as a force for good in the world."

> "In all of our country's history, there is no parallel to what President Obama and his former Secretary of State have done to weaken our nation."

> "...the message in the [prior] Administration's cutbacks: America is weaker and retreating."

"After nearly eight years of a Democratic Commander-in-Chief who has frequently placed strategic and ideological limitations and shackles on our military, our enemies have been emboldened and our national security is at great risk."

"Our U.S. Ambassador and American personnel were left without adequate security or backup halfway across the world in Benghazi."

"That sound consensus [support for Israel] was replaced with impotent grandstanding on the part of the current President and his Secretaries of State."

The GOP's position on immigration, even in 2016, was not consistent with the views of the majority of Americans. Only those whose fear and hatred was stirred by xenophobic rhetoric watched the long-established and slowly evolving immigration policy in anger and disgust.

The Republican Party's narrative that US interests and prestige on the world stage had been diminished by a Democratic administration were well reflected in its platform. But no evidence was offered in support of the accusation, and the posturing of a military strongman was tacitly offered as a solution.

The mention of Benghazi was a tip of the hat to those who had succumbed to the conspiracy theories spun around the event; by 2016 even the GOP knew better.

~

Proving that the GOP has no exclusive rights to straw man arguments, the Democratic Party focuses more on the person of Donald Trump, rather than the party. Most prominently, the platform refers *seven times* to "President Trump's recession."

"For people who risk losing their insurance coverage if they lose their jobs in this pandemic and in President Trump's recession....."

"To prevent President Trump's recession from becoming a depression....."

"...small businesses may not survive President Trump's recession."

> "We will impose rigorous oversight on big corporations seeking financial assistance to weather the pandemic and President Trump's recession....."

> "President Trump's recession threatens to deepen existing inequities....."

> "Democrats believe the COVID-19 pandemic, and President Trump's recession, demand unprecedented, transformational federal investments....."

> "We will surge funding to the Indian Health Service and support investments to help Tribal governments address the economic fallout of the COVID-19 pandemic and President Trump's recession....."

Donald Trump cannot be held liable for the recession of 2020. Indeed, the Republican Party cannot be held to bear exclusive responsibility. The recession was made inevitable by fundamental errors of public policy that have been promoted, or at least tolerated, by both parties over decades. And if Trump himself made the economy even more vulnerable, most of the most damaging policies he promoted were sent to him by Congress. Additionally, the Covid-19 pandemic would have had negative economic consequences even if it had been handled competently by the current Republican administration.

Elsewhere, straw man arguments can be found when the Democratic platform attempts to impute motives for which there is little evidence.

> "President Trump's failure to pay attention to early intelligence reports about the pandemic wasted critical weeks in which we could have prepared for the outbreak."

The President is quite likely to have paid attention to early intelligence reports. His failure to act upon them might be attributed to a variety of motives, including perceived political expediency, cognitive dissonance, or malicious intent.

> "President Trump tried to divide us, using racist and xenophobic rhetoric that has contributed to an increase in hate crimes against Asian Americans and Pacific Islanders."

There is little evidence that the President's divisive words and acts arise from a desire to divide us. His behavior might be better explained by a diagnosis of sociopathy or psychopathy.

> "Our essential workers have been deemed expendable by the President and his Administration."

There is little evidence that the President or his administration ever made such a judgment. A more likely explanation lies in the possibility that the administration's inept policy response endangered essential workers.

~

Straw-man attacks are just one category of distortions found in the platforms. Other distortions may defy classification. The GOP makes some general assertions that distort the truth beyond recognition.

> "…[The] United States the world's freest and most prosperous nation."

The Organization for Economic Cooperation and Development (OECD) offers a customizable database with which you can evaluate for yourself your freedom as an American - the tool takes some of the subjectivity out of the question. However, the claim to the most prosperous nation is dubious. On a per-capita basis, it can be defended; America is home to the uber-wealthy. However, U.S. median wealth per adult is lower than many other countries. To be exact, it came in at #27 for 2012, at $38,786 per adult. This is according to Credit Suisse's Global Wealth Databook, and it's a function of the economic inequality rampant in America. For the vast majority of Americans, the US is nowhere near the most prosperous nation.

> "As the Director of the FBI has noted, it is not possible to vet fully all potential refugees."

This statement ignores the fact that it will *never* be possible to vet fully all potential refugees. To apply such a standard would be to effectively preclude any immigration by refugees or any other persons. This statement essentially set the table for the incumbent Republican administration's severe restrictions on immigration, refuge, and resident aliens.

> "…the IRS has become an ideological attack dog for the worst elements of today's Democratic Party."

This allegation ignores the facts of the IRS "scandal" - that the avalanche of 501(c)3 applications from the radical right - unleashed in the wake of *Citizens United v FEC* - came under scrutiny based on the wording of the filings.

> "The survival of the internet as we know it is at risk. Its gravest peril originates in the White House, the current [previous] occupant of which has launched a campaign, both at home and internationally, to subjugate it to agents of government."

This refers, of course, to the mission of the FCC to ensure an open Internet without discrimination or throttling by service providers. Prohibiting its abuse does not imperil the Internet.

> "We pledge to protect those business owners who have been subjected to hate campaigns, threats of violence, and other attempts to deny their civil rights."

Boycotts are an expression of a free people, not hate campaigns. Evidence of threats of violence against business owners is scanty, and is lacking here.

> "American businesses now face the world's highest corporate tax rates."

While the statutory tax rate for US corporations was at the top of developed economies in 2016, the effective rate - actually paid - was much lower. In 2003 US corporations paid 16.9% of income in federal income taxes, and that income would have been stated higher were it not for reduction through revenue recognition, depreciation, and inventory valuation - not to mention direct subsidies. Following the corporate tax cuts made effective in 2018, US corporations have enjoyed rates as low or lower than other developed nations - and they continue to enjoy subsidies on capital formation and deployment.

> "We are the party of the Declaration of Independence and the Constitution."

No party can claim these documents for themselves - the documents make it clear from the beginning that they are by and for "we the people."

"No other nation has been as generous with food aid to the needy."

Foreign food aid is structured as a subsidy for American food producers. Taxpayers pay agribusiness corporations to send food to needy countries. Markets for food production and distribution in the destination countries are severely disrupted and rendered increasingly dependent on imports from American producers.

"Thirty years ago, the world's estimated reserves of oil were 645 billion barrels. Today, that figure is 1.65 trillion barrels."

The GOP claim implies that reserves are increasing - not consumption - and that there's no need to develop alternative energy sources. Industry sources estimate that reserves will last between 38 and 51 more years at current rates of extraction and consumption. However, the rate of consumption is on a sharply increasing trend, and as reserves are depleted extraction becomes slower and more expensive. [4]

"Their [American higher education institutions] excellence is undermined by an ideological bias deeply entrenched within the current university system."

Bias is so subjective as to be a meaningless basis for attack. What was lacking was any basis or support for the assertion.

"Any honest agenda for improving health care must start with repeal of the dishonestly named Affordable Care Act of 2010: Obamacare."

Honest? Really, GOP?

"A Republican commander-in-chief will protect the religious freedom of all military members, especially chaplains, and will not tolerate attempts to ban Bibles or religious symbols from military facilities."

A GOP President was called here to respond to an urban myth representing an imagined threat - no serious attempt has ever been made to ban Christian propaganda from military facilities. [5]

"We reject the false notion that Israel is an occupier and specifically recognize that the Boycott, Divestment, and Sanctions Movement (BDS) is anti-Semitic in nature and seeks to destroy Israel."

The referenced notion is deemed false without support, and the motives of the BDS movement are imputed incorrectly.

> "The current [prior] Administration's "opening to Cuba" was a shameful accommodation to the demands of its tyrants."

This assertion is presented without evidence, and imputes motive.

> "We reject the Democrats' approach of rationing inherent in Obamacare."

Health care is not an infinite resource, and therefore can never be in infinite supply. The Affordable Care Act relies on a panel of medical professionals and a defined appeal process to allocate health care resources. The free market relies on money instead - if you don't have money for medical care you don't receive medical care. The 2016 GOP platform preferred the latter approach.

~

The Democratic Party platform engages in a degree of puffery. Its history and its record sometimes fail to support the way it describes itself, and its view of American values and practices is sometimes seen through the lens of the optimist. Here are the most prominent distortions of Democratic Party platform.

> "Americans believe that diversity is our greatest strength. That protest is among the highest forms of patriotism. That our fates and fortunes are bound to rise and fall together. That even when we fall short of our highest ideals, we never stop trying to build a more perfect union."

> "Out of many, we are one."

> "Hate and its symbols have no home in America."

> "And all Americans should benefit from the clean energy economy....."

These are values and ideals of the Democratic Party, not the values and ideals of a unified America. Uniformity and conformity is preferred to diversity by many conservatives of the southern tradition. Protest is seen as lawlessness by the authoritarian right. And corporate capitalists certainly wouldn't agree that our fortunes are tied together - and *they run the country.*

Hate and its symbols have long been mainstays of American tradition. Thousands of monuments to confederate generals dot the landscape from the tip of Florida to the plains of Wisconsin. The battle flag of the Army of Northern Virginia is flown, even 155 years after its defeat.

There are those who would not realize a net benefit from a clean energy economy. Executives and shareholders of fossil fuel companies stand to lose wealth to clean energy. And these folks have enormous influence over today's public policy.

The Democratic Party is projecting its values on greater America. If the past four years has taught us anything, it's that there are those among us in great numbers who do not share our values and ideals.

> "We must once again stop another Republican recession from becoming a second Great Depression."

> "President Trump and the Republican Party have rigged the economy in favor of the wealthiest few and the biggest corporations....."

> "Unlike President Trump, we will stand up to efforts from China and other state actors to steal America's intellectual property....."

To claim that the economic recession of 2020 is attributable to the Republican Party is a gross distortion. Decades of economic policy crafted by corporate interests have been facilitated by both major parties. Likewise, the economy may be rigged in favor of the wealthy and their corporations, but Trump and the Republican Party cannot bear the entire blame. To claim the President Trump has failed to stand against China's theft of intellectual property ignores the administrations direct engagement of the issue in both trade negotiations, tariffs, and the threat of blacklisting Chinese companies.

> "Democrats will keep up the fight until all Americans can access secure, affordable, high-quality health insurance - because as Democrats, we fundamentally believe health care is a right for all, not a privilege for the few."

This fails to distinguish between health insurance and health care. Providing health insurance for all may not provide health care for all.

> "Democrats believe we need to protect, strengthen, and build
> upon our bedrock health care programs, including the
> Affordable Care Act, Medicare, Medicaid, and the Veterans
> Affairs (VA) system."

Not all Democrats believe this. The entire liberal wing of the Party has called for the implementation of a national healthcare system based upon a universal coverage model like that which is enjoyed by seniors - *Medicare for All.* To claim that "Democrats believe" is a gross distortion, and fails to recognize the real schism between the moderate and liberal / progressive wings of the Party.

> "Democrats... and recognize that race-neutral policies are not
> sufficient to rectify race-based disparities."

This implies that Democrats know and can confront policies that are not race-neutral. History has proven that Democrats have failed to address the broader question of inequality and the fundamental causes thereof. Without addressing the fundamentals, affirmative action will only patch the underlying problem.

> "Democrats are committed to the sacred principle of 'one
> person, one vote'....."

The Electoral College says otherwise. Without dealing with the electoral system that's set in constitutional concrete, the principle of "one person one vote" is nothing more than a hollow phrase. In order to bring integrity to this plank, the Democratic Party must put forth a process to change the Electoral College system in a meaningful way.

> "The unequal treatment of Puerto Rico's residents must end."

There's a fundamental reason that Puerto Rico has been victimized. The Jones Act, passed one hundred years ago, requires goods shipped between U.S. ports to be transported on ships that are built, owned, and operated by United States citizens or permanent residents. [6] Since its inception, the law has cost Puerto Rico about the same as its public debt - about $75 billion today. [7] Mercantilist colonialism is alive and well, but it seems that the DNC doesn't understand how to fix it.

> "Educators have always been heroes."

> "Education is fundamental to the idea of America and to fulfilling our nation's promise."

> "Democrats believe that everyone should be able to earn a degree beyond high school, if they choose to, without money standing in the way."

Education is a contentious issue in America today. Educators may be worshipped as heroes until they demand fair pay, then they may be reviled as socialists. University professors are condemned by some as radicals when they promote free thought. Democrats may validly speak for themselves, but they may not speak for others; Republicans flatly declare that there is not valid role for the federal government in education.

Educators may disagree that everyone should be able to earn a degree beyond high school; they know that not everyone can do so unless they are indulged by a system that isn't genuinely conditioned on academic achievement.

> "President Trump promised he would put 'America First' - but Trump's America stands alone."

This is a gross oversimplification. While the leaders of many US allies have been personally alienated, they generally continue to stand together with us on matters of shared strategic interest. Other partnerships - including those with the governments of Saudi Arabia, Israel, Turkey, Brazil, Poland, and Russia - have been strengthened. A few relationships, such as those among the US, Mexico, and Canada, have been threatened and subsequently reconciled. But these global shifts of loyalty may be based more upon personal relationships than upon strategic interests, and are likely to realign upon a change in the US regime.

> "Rather than end our forever wars, [Trump has] brought us to the brink of new conflicts....."

Trump withdrew unilaterally from Syria, thus ending the years-long US presence there and yielding the field to Russian, Turkish, and Syrian forces.

> "Democrats believe that the United States has an urgent, moral obligation and strategic interest to help alleviate suffering around the globe."

The progressive / liberal wing of the Democratic Party has a decidedly isolationist streak. Although generally expressed with respect to trade, the Party is not united in favor of intervention to alleviate suffering, which is often accompanied by armed conflict.

Lies

A number of overt prevarications were ignored in the 2016 GOP platform if they were redundant, if they were relatively minor, or if they would have required many hours of research to document the deceit. But here's a partial list.

> "We pledge to restore the proper balance and vertical separation of powers between the federal government and state governments….."

States' rights is a dog whistle issue directed toward the racist faction of the Party. The lie was exposed with the deployment of unwanted federal police to the streets of blue-state cities by the incumbent Republican administration.

> "We respect the states' authority and flexibility to exclude abortion providers from federal programs such as Medicaid and other health care and family planning programs so long as they continue to… sell the body parts of aborted children."

Selling the body parts of aborted children is an urban myth created and promulgated by radical social conservatives who barely escaped prosecution for their effort. Repeating the lie in your political platform might be a worse lie.

> "The huge increase in the national debt demanded by and incurred during the current [prior] Administration…"

The national debt consists of its prior balance plus the annual deficits. The majority of the additional debt incurred since 2008 is a consequence of the financial collapse and associated impacts on revenues and expenditures. This statement ignored the role of the GOP in structuring the economy so that financial collapse was inevitable. More remarkably, the deficits incurred by the incumbent Republican administration stand in ironic judgment of this claim.

> "…the environmental establishment looks the other way when environmental degradation is caused by the EPA and other federal agencies as was the case during the Animas River spill."

The Animas River spill was a consequence of the EPA's effort to contain and remediate mineral pollution from mining above Silverton. To blame remediation efforts for the pollution itself is patently deceitful.

> "Information concerning a changing climate, especially projections into the long-range future, must be based on dispassionate analysis of hard data."

Really, GOP?

> "The current [prior] Administration's refusal to work with Republicans took our national debt from $10 trillion to nearly $19 trillion today."

On November 18, 2008, at the Caucus Room, and upscale Washington, DC restaurant, a meeting of Republican leadership was convened. Present were Newt Gingrich, Frank Luntz, Eric Cantor, Jeb Hensarling, Pete Hoekstra, Dan Lungren, Kevin McCarthy, Paul Ryan, Pete Sessions, Tom Coburn, Bob Corker, Jim DeMint, John Ensign and Jon Kyl. Together, they conspired to block anything and everything the new Administration attempted or proposed - regardless of the consequences to the national interest. The effort was largely successful, particularly regarding matters of budget and spending. To blame President Obama for refusal to work with Republicans was a big, carefully orchestrated, and oft-repeated lie.

> "…the [prior] Administration manufactured fiscal crises - phony government shutdowns - to demand excessive spending."

Ted Cruz led the campaign to defund Obamacare by holding government funding hostage in 2013. He said, "If we can actually get Republicans to stand up and fight, I believe we can win this fight." Victory was essential, given that they wouldn't get another shot at it. "No major entitlement, once it has been implemented, has ever been unwound," he said at the time. "If we don't do it now, in all likelihood we never will." Cruz didn't get Obamacare defunded, but he wasted 21 hours on the senate floor and at least $21 billion dollars in costs.

Only later did the GOP narrative try to shift the blame to President Obama. At the time, Cruz was quite proud of himself as a "fighter."

> "Government cannot create prosperity, though government can limit or destroy it."

Without comment - ask your favorite economist!

> "Competitiveness equals jobs."

Competitiveness equals operating efficiencies, which are generally described by the relationship of revenues to costs. One significant cost category is labor, and reducing labor increases the relationship of revenues to costs. Competitiveness usually equals reducing the cost of labor relative to revenues, and therefore equals cutting jobs.

> "The worst of Dodd-Frank is the Consumer Financial Protection Bureau, deliberately designed to be a rogue agency."

The CFPB was designed to be independent from political manipulation.

> "Diversion of settlement funds [from CFPB actions] to politically connected parties should be a criminal offense."

This implies that the CFPB is diverting settlement funds for political reasons, an allegation unsupported by evidence or compelling suspicion. Settlements are public, and subject to rigorous procedural requirements. [8]

> "Ongoing attempts to compel individuals, businesses, and institutions of faith to transgress their beliefs are part of a misguided effort to undermine religion and drive it from the public square."

Oh, puh-leeze!

> "Places of worship for the first time in our history have reason to fear the loss of tax-exempt status merely for espousing and practicing traditional religious beliefs that have been held across the world for thousands of years, and for almost four centuries in America."

Since 1954, US tax code has prevented 501(c) organizations from conducting political campaign activities while enjoying an exemption as a non-profit organization. Regulations are clear - a church's tax status cannot be endangered by espousing religious beliefs. [9]

> "Limits on political speech [by limiting money influence] serve only to protect the powerful and insulate incumbent officeholders."

No evidence was offered for this patently false statement. Unlimited money influence best serves those candidates and parties that represent those with the most money - plutocrats, corporations, and wealthy individuals.

> "The confirmation to the Court of additional anti-gun justices would eviscerate the Second Amendment's fundamental protections."

Eviscerate?

> "We condemn frivolous lawsuits against gun manufacturers and the current [prior] Administration's illegal harassment of firearm dealers."

Wounded victims and family members of those murdered with guns do not regard their lawsuits as frivolous.

> "We oppose the use of public funds to perform or promote abortion or to fund organizations, like Planned Parenthood, so long as they provide or refer for elective abortions or sell fetal body parts rather than provide health care."

The allegation that abortion providers sold off body parts is an urban myth, and when used as a plank in a party platform it was a lie.

> "...the American people [have] the world's best health care."

This is a whopper. The US actually ranks last among the 11 wealthiest nations of the world. [10] And the recent pandemic has exposed its latent vulnerabilities.

> "An unconstitutional effort to impose National Popular Vote would be a grave threat to our federal system and a guarantee of corruption, as every ballot box in every state would offer a chance to steal the presidency."

There is nothing unconstitutional about this initiative; the Electoral College is a nexus for manipulation and corruption, both domestic and foreign.

> "During the last eight years of a Democratic Administration, nearly all the work requirements for able-bodied adults, instituted by our landmark welfare reform of 1996, have been removed." "…the current [prior] Administration has nullified any meaningful work requirement and made TANF a mockery of the name we gave it:"

The [prior] Administration had done neither, but merely granted states the right to petition to modify TANF requirements to meet local needs. Even so the lie appeared twice in the GOP platform [11].

> "We have been fighting the War on Poverty for 50 years and poverty is winning. Our social safety net - about 80 separate means-tested programs costing over $1 trillion every year - is designed to help people born into or falling into poverty."

Medicaid, Medicare, food stamps, Head Start, and Job Corps are still functional today. However the GOP dismantled key components of the program in the early seventies and in 1981, essentially declaring a truce in the War on Poverty as the War on Poor was declared. [12]

> "Over-regulation is the quiet tyranny of the 'Nanny State.' It hamstrings American businesses and hobbles economic growth."

As of 2016, the United States actually ranked 7th out of 189 world economies for being the least burdensome in the world. [13]

> "Cronyism is inherent in the progressive vision of the administrative state."

> "Poverty, not wealth, is the gravest threat to the environment….."

Seriously?

> "Federal ownership or management of land also places an economic burden on counties and local communities in terms of lost revenue to pay for things such as schools, police, and emergency services."

Academic studies not funded by special interests refute this unfounded assertion. Typical of these studies is Holmes and Hecox. [14]

> "A good understanding of the Bible being indispensable for the development of an educated citizenry....."

This faith-based belief is offered as fact; as such it is simply a lie.

> "That approach [abstinence indoctrination] - the only one always effective against premarital pregnancy and sexually-transmitted disease - empowers teens to achieve optimal health outcomes."

This is false. Where abstinence indoctrination replaces real sex education, STD rates and unwanted pregnancies have increased.

> "We assert that private [land] ownership has been the best guarantee of conscientious [environmental] stewardship....."

The National Park Service, Bureau of Land Management, the US Forest Service, and other public land ownership agencies offer evidence to the contrary.

~

The Democratic Party platform, while long on contradictions and distortions, was more careful with outright lies. But there are a few.

> "Friends and foes alike neither admire nor fear President Trump's leadership - they dismiss and ridicule it."

Many world leaders fear the leadership of President Trump, and for good reason. Friends like America's Kurdish allies in Syria were abandoned to their Syrian, Russian, and Turkish foes when US forces were abruptly withdrawn. Others fear the sociopathy that have de-stabilized relationships among trading partners and NATO allies. Authoritarian leaders the world over such as Andrzej Duda, Rodrigo Duterte, and Jair Bolsonaro do not dismiss Trump's leadership; instead they admire and emulate his rhetoric, strategies, and policies.

> "We cannot hope to raise wages without taking on the profound racial biases at work in our employment system."

Raising wages and reducing racial bias have both been on the Democratic Party's agenda for a very long time. But although they are related, they are separate planks. Wages can be raised with a variety of strategies that have nothing to do with racial bias. Increasing the minimum wage, for example, can be accomplished even while tolerating race-based practices in hiring and promotion.

Why Lie?

Why do political parties lie? Political parties are made up of people and other organizations that are themselves made up of people. *People lie*, so we can expect the organizations they create to lie too. But *why do people lie?*

Robert Feldman, PhD, a professor of psychology at University of Massachusetts Amherst, studies "verbal deceit." [15] He says that the biggest reason people are dishonest is simple - *lying works*. Let's look at some of the things we can accomplish by lying and see if that explains some of the planks in political platforms.

To get others to do what we want

First, we lie to get others to do what we want them to do. If we can't get what we want from others by other means, we might resort to deceit.

To flatter people

Feldman says flattery is one of the most common forms of deceit. We're often skeptical of flattery because we know it's not always sincere. Someone may give you a false compliment to befriend you, avoid awkwardness, persuade you to do them a favor, get you to confide in them, and more.

To avoid awkwardness

Nobody likes to be put in an uncomfortable position. So we sometimes use little lies to avoid disclosing our laziness, weakness, or dislike for people or situations we find uncomfortable. We all want to be liked by others and to not disappoint anyone.

To influence others

We've seen that we might lie to get others to act. But we may also lie to get others to agree with our positions or beliefs. Social media is a showcase for deceptions of this kind.

To avoid a negative outcome

Children often claim, "I didn't do it," to avoid blame or responsibility for something they know was wrong. Parents may see that it's an obvious lie, but as we get older we hone our skills to deceive more credibly.

To achieve a positive outcome

We may lie just to get what we want. Taking some unearned deductions on our tax return might get us a bigger refund.

To make ourselves look more impressive

Many of us aspire to be better than we are. Others of wish were not as bad as we are. Either way, we might use aspirational lies to get others to view us as we would like to be seen.

To maintain a previous lie

When we first lie about something small initially, we might have to maintain that lie by lying in bigger and bigger ways.

So that's why people lie. Can we discern similar motivations in the platforms of political parties? We've seen that a party's purpose, stripped of its ideology and its rhetoric, is to gain and maintain power over public policy. Parties accomplish this by influencing us so that we can be persuaded to do what they want us to do.

They may use flattery by telling us that our shared values are pure and noble.

They may deny responsibility for past mistakes, or even blame others for their failures.

They may repeat the most preposterous lies - *our lies* - to keep our loyalty.

They may tell little aspirational lies to make themselves look better than they are, or they may tell dark and dirty whoppers to make their policies seem less destructive than they are.

They may tell a continuous series of new lies to perpetuate an original lie embedded in long-embraced economic policies.

And they may avoid awkwardness simply by failing to publish any policy platform at all.

Amid the deep and growing division between sectors of the American populace, one common theme emerges - we all feel increasingly left out. We are fearful that others will gain an advantage over us, and our political parties may encourage us to believe that they already have. As our fear turns into rage, it's increasingly directed toward *the other* - other countries, other races, other states, other genders, other religions - *any other* will do.

There are real reasons for many of us to feel left out - *we are left out.* Economic inequality has concentrated wealth in America to a greater degree than at any time in nearly a century. This inequality is a valid target for the fear and rage so many people feel. And yet, the rage is rarely directed toward the corporations that bring us the goods we love to consume, and seldom do we attack the "job creators" that constitute the wealthy class and who really do provide many of us with employment. Individually, after all, corporations and wealthy people are innocently enjoying the fruits of a system that rewards their enterprise.

And there's the lie! Yes, corporations and wealthy people may be individually innocent, but they are the beneficiaries of a system that has been rigged - *corrupted to the core* - in their favor. Individually, they may have had nothing to do with the rigging, but somebody has done it. And we can't blame either of today's political parties, because the corruption goes back hundreds of years.

But one party *champions* the cause of corporations and wealthy people. And with increasing levels of economic inequality, such a party would be vulnerable indeed if popular rage were directed against the factors that actually create and sustain inequality. The very survival of such a party would depend upon its success in redirecting that popular rage and vectoring it toward the other - *any other.*

And the party has help - *lots of help* - from corporate media. Chris Hedges says that today's news organizations, controlled by their corporate owners, focus their influence [16] on a single mission - to redirect the dissatisfaction and outrage of those suffering from corporatism to less threatening targets. For example, lower wages are said to be a result of illegal immigration, not employment policy. Unemployment is said to be a result of regulations that penalize job creators, not the practices of outsourcing and offshoring. And rising food costs are said to be a result of government food regulation, not the ever-increasing profits of corporate farms.

But both parties lie, don't they? Sure. We are a species that lies, living in a culture that lies, listening to corporate media that lies - all because self-interest demands that we seek every advantage in an increasingly competitive world.

So expect to see and hear lies, but prepare yourself to recognize them so that you can act - *and vote* - according to your own actual self-interests.

[1] http://bidnessetcnews.tumblr.com/post/144449681606/bankruptcies-in-the-energy-sector-past-present

[2] https://www.opednews.com/articles/Trump-s-Economy--It-s-a-F-by-Larry-Butler-Corporations_Economy_Economy-Recession_Economy-Economics--US-200124-178.html

[3] http://www.nytimes.com/2014/01/30/us/politics/house-approves-farm-bill-ending-2-year-impasse.html

[4] http://www.ibtimes.co.uk/world-energy-day-2014-how-much-oil-left-how-long-will-it-last-1471200

[5] https://www.truthorfiction.com/gideons-military-bases/

[6] https://www.investopedia.com/terms/j/jonesact.asp

[7] https://www.opednews.com/articles/Colonialism-at-Work-in-Pue-by-Larry-Butler-Caribbean-Islands_Colonialism_Colonialism_Community-Of-Latin-American-And-Caribbean-States-C-160418-256.html

[8] https://www.venable.com/cfpb-enforcement-settlement-principles-revealed-03-22-2016/

[9] https://www.irs.gov/pub/irs-pdf/p4220.pdf

[10] http://www.commonwealthfund.org/~/media/files/publications/fund-report/2014/jun/1755_davis_mirror_mirror_2014.pdf

[11] http://www.factcheck.org/2012/08/does-obamas-plan-gut-welfare-reform/

[12] https://www.washingtonpost.com/news/wonk/wp/2014/01/08/everything-you-need-to-know-about-the-war-on-poverty/

[13] http://acetool.commerce.gov/regulatory-compliance-costs

[14] http://www.wilderness.net/library/documents/IJWDec04_Holmes.pdf

[15] https://www.health.com/mind-body/why-do-people-lie

[16] https://www.truthdig.com/articles/chris-hedges-on-the-disintegrated-media-cultural-illiteracy/

Who Wins?

Which platform wins the great Platform War of 2020? Answer: If you want to win a war, you've got to show up to do battle. But this election cycle, the GOP is MIA - *missing in action.*

GOP is MIA

The decision of the Republican National Committee's Executive Committee on June 10, 2020, to adopt the same platform the party used in 2016 is unprecedented in modern political history. Within the context of today's social, economic, and political upheaval, the passive approach is stunning. We're living in a very different country than we were four years ago, and yet the RNC chose to dust off the 2016 platform and let it ride.

Why? The official Website of the Republican National Committee [1] is mute on the subject, offering no explanation whatsoever that the old platform has been carried forward without any revisions at all - *not even the year "2016" printed on the cover page.*

But others speak out. Republican Party officials and influencers justify the action - or *inaction* - in various ways.

> Justin Clark, senior counsel for the Trump campaign: "President Trump won in 2016 with this platform and he'll win again in 2020 with this platform."
>
> Colleen Holcomb, president of the Eagle Forum: "Given the quarantine situation, we were concerned that decisions regarding the Platform not be made in proverbial smoke-filled rooms or through secret meetings in Washington, D.C." [2]
>
> [A] GOP operative close to the Trump campaign said the only people "who actually think the platform matters are naive," while adding that most state Republican parties and county GOP chapters have their own platforms that local and state officials pay closer attention to. [3]

Other GOP party officials and influencers disagree.

Terry Schilling, executive director of American Principles Project: "We can't go into 2020 with the same platform we had in 2016, and by limiting the ability to make changes you run the risk of having a stale platform. It will be tone deaf."

Jennifer Williams, 2016 national delegate: "Anything positive that the Trump administration has achieved in the last three years can't be put into this document now because this document is frozen..... It's very sloppy to do it this way." [4]

Jerri Ann Henry, former executive director of Log Cabin Republicans, said the decision effectively upholds "one of the worst platforms in terms of LGBT issues..... I would have loved to have seen them say, 'Alright, that didn't work, so let's try to root out the issues.' Going from one big attempt to consolidate the platform to keeping the 2016 platform is just a big punt," she said in an interview Thursday, adding that reusing the 2016 platform is "in no way, shape, form or fashion … an OK solution." [5]

So we have the divergent views from within the Republican Party itself. And they come from all over the red part of the political spectrum. So what gives? What are the real reasons?

"The Republican Party has not yet voted on a Platform," Trump said in a morning tweet. "No rush. I prefer a new and updated Platform, short form, if possible." [6]

"The full platform is still essential for guiding policy, holding legislators accountable, and for distinguishing policy differences between Republicans and Democrats," the Eagle Forum had written..... "We respectfully request that all efforts to streamline the overall platform, which has been forged over more than a century of committed grassroots activism, be resisted."

RNC National press secretary Mandi Merritt blamed the situation on North Carolina Gov. Roy Cooper, a Democrat, who has rejected the party's plans for a full-fledged convention in his state. "His refusal to work with the RNC on holding a full event in his state left our members with no choice. It would not be right for a very small group to craft a new platform without all of the delegates present," Merritt said in a statement. [7]

What Do Others Say?

A Platform Would be Trashed Anyway

The Republican Party understands that policy is being defined and implemented on the fly by a leader that flaunts tradition, ignores the advice of political veterans. The Party has allowed this hijacking of doctrine because it realizes that it serves the interests of those who control the Party. In fact, many of the most extreme and outrageous policy initiatives of the incumbent administration - such as the use of private border prisons - confer financial gain on the Party's benefactors.

Nepotism and Discord Couldn't Resolved in Time

The son-in-law of the President, Jared Kushner, was tasked with overhauling the 2016 GOP platform in May, 2020. The platform had been under review for several months by then, and Kushner's involvement imposed an entirely different paradigm upon the project. Kushner's goal was to reduce the entire 2016 platform, updated, to a manifesto that could be printed on a not card. He envisioned the listing of *ten principles that Republicans believe in.*

We've seen that the Republican Party consists of an assortment of special interests bound by the enabling power of corporate capital at the center. The issues of each of these special interests were well considered in the 58-page 2016 GOP platform, as we have seen. There is simply not enough space on a note card to provide for numerous parochial interests. Objections to the short version were led by a coalition of Evangelical, Dominionist, Fundamentalist, Christian religious-liberty Republicans whose mutual support has been a feature of conservative politics for eight decades.

Internal Conflicts Developed Over Unpopular Issues

Even though the 2016 GOP platform was written just four years ago, its values and policies were regarded by moderates as archaic. Worse yet, some were expected to cost votes. Internal conflicts over same-sex marriage and civil rights simply couldn't be resolved in a party torn asunder by extremist views and ad-hoc leadership.

What Can a Party Say?

A platform that addressed current issues would have to deal with Covid-19 handling, a family separation policy, extraordinary levels of political corruption, foreign interference in elections, and the use of militarized force against peaceful protesters. It's likely that party bosses recognized that there was no way to deal with these issues without admitting the failures of the incumbent administration. Without facing the issues, there would be no possible way to craft policy solutions to address them.

Who's In Charge Here?

The Republican Party, in failing to state its values, principles, and policies clearly in its traditional platform, has abdicated its primary role. The Party has surrendered its soul to the most corrupt leader it has ever served.

~

Democrats Show Up

Democrats win the Platform Wars of 2020 by a score of 91 to zero.

In its ninety-one pages, the 2020 Democratic Party platform engages nearly all of America's most pressing public policy issues with explicit statements of value, principle, belief, and policy.

The DNC acknowledges the reality of a global pandemic that will leave an indelible mark on US history and proposes that science and medicine drive public policy.

The Party acknowledges that election interference is a factor, but makes a weak case for taking action against the illegal attacks by Russian interests.

The Party acknowledges the reality of today's civil unrest while endorsing the values of the Black Lives Matter movement and condemning the use of even more repressive policing.

The Party acknowledges the tragedy of the administration's family separation policy and offers both short- and long-term solutions as immigration reform.

The Party leaves no doubt about its commitment to universal equality of opportunity. It applies a simple test to equal rights under a Democratic administration: if you're a person you'll enjoy human rights; if you're a US citizen, you'll enjoy civil rights.

The Party proposes a variety of clean energy initiatives, even while avoiding labeling it a *green new deal.*

The Party wants law and order like all Americans, but prefers to address the root causes of lawlessness - poverty, addiction, and mental illness - rather than increasing enforcement and incarceration.

The Party leaves no doubt that it will spend more to make America a better place to live for its people. But it barely touches on the revenue side of the equation, and leaves the question, *"...how are we going to pay for it?"* unaddressed and unanswered.

In Summary

If political parties are like people, it's clear that Republicans are a little mixed up, and they're not what they want you to think they are. They certainly have inner conflicts, and possibly unstated ideals and goals. Never have those ideals and goals been *more unstated* than they are in a platform that simply doesn't exist. They're influenced by things going on around them - *even in the Whitehouse* - and they have a powerful instinct for survival.

If a party's platform is its ideal, the Republican Party has lost the vision to which it aspires. In contrast, the Democratic Party platform was carefully put together by political professionals to promote unity among its diverse members and followers.

If a party's platform is its conscience, its platform will tend to guide its politicians back to its own path over time. A party without a platform is a party without a conscience. A highly detailed platform reveals a willingness to explicitly commit to values, principles, and policies, even as certain policies may remain unstated.

If a party's platform can be corrupted, the most *benign sort of corruption* is its natural evolution in response to changing realities. However, *the greatest corruption* is to surrender the platform itself to the rule of a single man in order to maintain the party's power.

[1] https://www.gop.com/

[2] https://ballotpedia.org/The_Republican_Party_Platform,_2020

[3] https://www.politico.com/news/2020/06/11/republicans-rnc-decision-314172

[4] https://ballotpedia.org/The_Republican_Party_Platform,_2020

[5] https://www.politico.com/news/2020/06/11/republicans-rnc-decision-314172

[6] https://www.washingtonpost.com/politics/trump-calls-for-a-new-and-updated-gop-platform-after-party-moves-to-keep-its-2016-document/2020/06/12/f5d033cc-acb4-11ea-9063-e69bd6520940_story.html

[7] https://www.politico.com/news/2020/06/11/republicans-rnc-decision-314172

Afterword

Blind Spots

And what have both parties missed that might really matter? Let's follow the money. Every page of both platforms carries monetary and fiscal consequences. And if we follow the money we might discern the overt and hidden motivations - *and even the identities* - of those acting upon them.

For centuries, economic growth has been hobbled by the cost of subsidies for capital and capitalists. From reduced income tax rates for capital gains, qualified dividends, real estate interest and deferred income to direct subsidies for capital investments, and incentives for accounting tomfoolery and tax evasion - these are very real economic costs. And there are real, fundamental solutions to these problems. But one party sees them not as problems, but rather opportunities; the other party offers an assortment of patches and fixes that barely rise above the noise of attack-dog politics. The real, fundamental, durable solution would be to stop subsidizing capital and let it look out after its own interests. Do we think capitalism can't stand on its own two feet after thousands of years of dominance?

For decades, economic growth has been hobbled by the direct penalty on the employment of labor in the form of payroll taxes. Social Security was the centerpiece of Franklin Roosevelt's New Deal. Payroll taxes raise the cost of labor. Higher labor costs make employers less inclined to hire people and more inclined to seek alternatives to hiring - alternatives like automation, outsourcing, and offshoring.

Taxing payrolls has been public policy for more than eighty years, and today raises the cost of labor by about 16%. This has had a profound impact on the US economy, and all by itself accounts for much of the unemployment and suppressed wages we have today. The response of one party is to promote increases in the subsidies paid to corporate *job creators*. The response of the other party is for the government to expand a patchwork of complex safety net programs for those who fall through. Neither party offers realistic solutions. The real, fundamental, durable solution would be to stop taxing the employment of labor and let supply and demand find a new equilibrium.

One party seems to exist for the purpose of guarding the public policies that favor capital over labor; the other party seems to exist for the purpose of creating patches and fixes for an economy that has been thus corrupted. And neither party seems to recognize the damage they wreak on the economic well-being of Americans.

It's all right there, in black and white, in the platforms for all to see.

Finding Common Ground

America is divided. And its divisions show up clearly in the camps of the parties that purport to represent us. But we have noted a few areas of agreement. Are these a valid place to start if we wish to unite as a country?

Declaration of Independence states, ""We hold these truths to be self-evident, that all men are created equal, that they are endowed by their Creator with certain unalienable Rights, that among these are Life, Liberty and the pursuit of Happiness."

Americans universally cherish life, liberty, and the pursuit of happiness. We value security from assault both individually and as a nation. We value the freedom of our press, even as that freedom might irritate our sensibilities. We want peace; and for many decades Americans have enjoyed freedom from the death and destruction of war in our homeland. We value the service of our men and women in uniform even when we object to their deployment. We care for the veterans of military service, especially if they have been wounded in the line of duty. We recognize the importance of job and career training, even if we prefer that the federal government stay out of it. And we're all united in the call for taxation that is at once fair, low, efficient, and sufficient to provide for government services.

Can we build unity out of these shared values?

The Author

Larry Judson Butler

Photo credit: Steve Grove, Photo Warrior

A career in banking, small-business operations, finance, and marketing gave him a view of business - and the world - by the numbers. He shared his perspective in a modest consulting practice and in his university classroom.

An early retirement gave him a chance to travel the country for more than fifteen years. He saw for himself the rising economic inequality around us and the desperate poverty it breeds. A growing appreciation of American history and the political science that shaped it helped illuminate the people, places, and things he explored. A friend described him as a recovering CFO.

He continues to travel the country by motorhome and motorcycle, seeing old friends, making new ones, and marveling at the wonders of America and its people. His other books include...

Saving American Capitalism

Platform Wars - Do YOU Know What Your Party is Up To?

Originalism & Justice - and Other Conservative Lies

Talk About Poverty - A Meal for Your Story

Corporate Capital's War on America

Tax Reform for Donkeys - How Democrats Can Get it Right